Life Coach Guide for

Busy Mums

By Sommer Currie

Contents

Preface

Thank you for choosing the "Life Coach Guide for Busy Mums." My name is Sommer Currie, and I am an empowerment life coach dedicated to helping women find balance, joy, and fulfilment in their busy lives. The inspiration behind this book stems from my extensive experience working with women who strive to make the most of their time amidst the demands of motherhood and career.

If you're like me, you'll understand the challenges of juggling professional aspirations and the responsibilities of raising children. Before having my son, I was intensely career-driven, and while that ambition remained, I had to navigate a significant transition to find a new balance. At 40, I welcomed my son into the world, and the shift was nothing short of transformative. The change was profound in terms of lifestyle and learning to manage time and expectations in an entirely new context. It took a considerable time to adjust, find my footing, and thrive again.

This book is designed as a comprehensive guide to help busy mums, particularly those navigating the complexities of midlife motherhood. We will explore a wide array of topics, all aimed at empowering you to live your best life. From celebrating the milestones of your birthdays and embracing youthful vitality to incorporating holistic wellness practices and maintaining a balanced diet, this guide will cover the essential areas of life coaching that I use in my practice.

In our journey together, we will delve into strength and fitness routines tailored for busy schedules, and strategies for planning nutritious meals that support your health and energy levels. This book is a distillation of my empowerment life coaching program, adapted to meet the unique needs of busy mums who are determined to have it all.

Balancing career and motherhood are no small feat. It requires resilience, adaptability, and a commitment to self-care. My goal is to provide you with practical tips and actionable advice that can help you navigate this path with confidence and grace. Whether you're looking to carve out time for meditation, stay healthy and youthful, or find new ways to manage your time effectively, "Life Coach Guide for Busy Mums" is here to support you.

I understand that every mother's journey is unique, and the path to balance and fulfilment will look different for each of us. This book is not about prescribing a one-size-fits-all solution but rather offering a toolkit of strategies that you can adapt to fit your own life. From time management techniques to self-care rituals, we'll explore a variety of approaches to help you find what works best for you.

As we embark on this journey together, I encourage you to be kind to yourself and patient with the process. Change doesn't happen overnight, but with persistence and the right mindset, you can create a life that feels balanced, joyful, and fulfilling. Remember, you are not alone in this journey. There are countless mums out there who are navigating similar challenges, and together, we can support and inspire one another to achieve our goals.

Thank you for allowing me to be a part of your journey. Let's embrace the changes, celebrate our milestones, and strive to live our best lives as empowered, busy mums.

Chapter 1: The Transformative Power of Meditation

Welcome to a journey designed just for you, a busy mum who's balancing it all, but still craves a little more joy, peace, and fulfilment in life. This book is here to offer practical, relatable advice to help you nurture yourself while juggling your many roles. Together, we'll explore ways to make your life easier, more fulfilling, and yes, even more fun!

One of the first tools we'll dive into is meditation, a simple but powerful way to enhance your mental and emotional well-being. It's perfect for mums like us who are constantly on the go. We'll talk about how you can easily slip meditation into your day no matter how hectic and the lasting benefits it brings to your overall happiness and sense of calm. Take it from me, even just 10 minutes before bed can do wonders for your mindset. And if you're not sure how to start, don't worry, I've got you covered!

Understanding Meditation

What is Meditation?

Let's be real—life as a mum can feel like a never-ending to-do list. Between juggling work, the idea of finding time to meditate might sound like one more thing to add to the pile. But here's the thing: meditation isn't some mystical, far-off practice reserved for monks or yogis on mountain tops. It's really just about hitting the pause button on all that mental chatter and giving yourself a break, even if it's just for a few minutes.

Imagine this: the children are napping, you've got five minutes to yourself (a miracle, right?), and instead of scrolling on your phone, you sit quietly, breathe deeply, and just be. Meditation is like a mental power nap, helping you clear away distractions, focus, and find a tiny slice of calm in the chaos.

Do you want to know the best part? You don't need hours of free time or a fancy setup; you can meditate in your living room, your car (parked, of course!), or even while folding laundry. And the benefits? Backed by science and history—thousands of years of it! At its core, meditation is about mindfulness—just being present and tuning into your thoughts and feelings without letting them run wild. No need for perfection, no need to judge yourself.

So, don't stress about mastering meditation; just start with a few deep breaths and see how a little peace can ripple through the rest of your day. You've got this!

Types of Meditation

There are several types of meditation, each with its unique techniques and benefits. Some of the most popular forms include:

1. **Mindfulness Meditation:** This form of meditation involves paying attention to your thoughts and feelings without judging them. It is often practised by focusing on the breath and observing the mind's activity.
2. **Guided Meditation:** In guided meditation, a guide or teacher leads you through the meditation process, often using visualisation techniques to help you relax and focus.
3. **Transcendental Meditation:** This technique involves silently repeating a mantra – a specific word or phrase – to help the mind settle into a state of restful alertness.
4. **Loving-Kindness Meditation (Metta):** This practice focuses on developing feelings of compassion and love towards oneself and others.
5. **Body Scan Meditation:** This involves focusing on different parts of the body and becoming aware of any sensations or tension.

Mental Health Benefits

Meditation has a profound impact on mental health. Regular practice can lead to significant improvements in various aspects of mental well-being, including:

1. **Reduced Stress:** Meditation helps to lower cortisol levels, the body's primary stress hormone. This can lead to a decrease in overall stress levels and help manage the symptoms of chronic stress.

2. **Improved Focus and Concentration:** By training the mind to stay focused on the present moment, meditation enhances attention span and cognitive function.
3. **Enhanced Emotional Health:** Meditation can improve mood and increase emotional resilience, making it easier to cope with life's challenges.
4. **Decreased Anxiety and Depression:** Regular meditation practice has been shown to reduce symptoms of anxiety and depression by promoting a more positive outlook on life and improving emotional regulation.
5. **Better Sleep:** Meditation can help relax the mind and body, making it easier to fall asleep and improve sleep quality.

Physical Health Benefits

In addition to mental health benefits, meditation also contributes to physical well-being:

- **Lower Blood Pressure:** By promoting relaxation, meditation helps to lower blood pressure and improve cardiovascular health.
- **Reduced Pain:** Meditation can enhance pain tolerance and reduce the perception of pain by altering the way the brain processes pain signals.
- **Strengthened Immune System:** Regular meditation practice can boost the immune system, making the body more resilient to illnesses.
- **Improved Digestion:** The relaxation response triggered by meditation can improve digestion and reduce symptoms of gastrointestinal disorders.

Incorporating Meditation into a Busy Schedule

Finding time to meditate can be challenging, especially for us mums juggling multiple responsibilities. However, even a few minutes of meditation each day can make a significant difference. Here are some practical tips for incorporating meditation into your daily routine:

Make It a Priority

To make meditation a regular part of your life, it's essential to prioritise it. Schedule it into your day as you would any other important activity. Whether it's first thing in the morning, during a lunch break, or before bed, find a time that works best for you and stick to it.

Start Small

If you're new to meditation, start with just a few minutes each day and gradually increase the duration as you become more comfortable with the practice. Even 5 to 10 minutes of meditation can have a positive impact on your well-being.

Use Guided Meditations

Guided meditations can be particularly helpful for beginners. They provide structure and support, making it easier to focus and relax. Many apps and websites offer free guided meditations, such as Mindful.org, which provides a comprehensive guide on how to meditate.

Create a Comfortable Space

Find a quiet, comfortable space where you won't be disturbed. It doesn't need to be elaborate – a simple corner of a room with a cushion or chair will do. The key is to create an environment that is conducive to relaxation and focus.

Integrate Meditation with Daily Activities

You don't always need to set aside a specific time for meditation. You can integrate mindfulness into your daily activities, such as while washing dishes, taking a shower, or walking. Focus on your breath and the sensations you're experiencing, and bring your attention back to the present moment whenever your mind starts to wander.

Be Patient and Persistent

Like any new habit, meditation takes time and practice to develop. Be patient with yourself and don't get discouraged if you find it difficult at first. The benefits of meditation become more apparent with consistent practice, so keep at it even if progress seems slow.

Meditation Techniques and Exercises

Here are some simple meditation techniques and exercises that you can incorporate into your daily routine:

Mindful Breathing

Find a comfortable position: Sit or lie down in a comfortable position with your back straight and your hands resting on your lap or by your sides.

- **Close your eyes:** Gently close your eyes and take a few deep breaths.
- **Focus on your breath:** Bring your attention to your breath. Notice the sensation of the air entering and leaving your nostrils, the rise and fall of your chest, and the expansion and contraction of your abdomen.
- **Count your breaths:** To help maintain focus, you can count each breath. Inhale and mentally count "one," exhale and count "two," and so on up to ten. Then start over from one.
- **Refocus your mind:** Whenever your mind starts to wander, gently bring your attention back to your breath.

Body Scan Meditation

Lie down or sit comfortably: Find a comfortable position where you can relax without being disturbed.

- **Close your eyes and breathe deeply:** Take a few deep breaths to help you relax.
- **Focus on different parts of your body:** Starting from your toes, slowly bring your attention to each part of your body, moving upwards towards your head. Notice any sensations, tension, or discomfort in each area.
- **Release tension:** As you focus on each part of your body, consciously relax and release any tension you're holding. Imagine the tension melting away with each exhale.
- **Complete the scan:** Once you've scanned your entire body, take a few moments to lie still and enjoy the feeling of relaxation.

Loving-Kindness Meditation

Find a comfortable position: Sit or lie down in a comfortable position with your back straight and your hands resting on your lap or by your sides.

- **Close your eyes and breathe deeply:** Take a few deep breaths to help you relax.
- **Generate feelings of love and compassion:** Bring to mind someone you love and imagine sending them feelings of love and compassion. You can use phrases such as "May you be happy," "May you be healthy," "May you be safe," and "May you live with ease."
- **Extend these feelings to yourself:** After a few minutes, turn your attention to yourself and repeat the same phrases. "May I be happy," "May I be healthy," "May I be safe," "May I live with ease."
- **Expand your focus:** Gradually expand your focus to include others in your life, such as friends, family, colleagues, and even people you may have conflicts with. Extend the same wishes of love and compassion to each person.

Guided Imagery Meditation

1. **Find a comfortable position:** Sit or lie down in a comfortable position with your back straight and your hands resting on your lap or by your sides.
2. **Close your eyes and breathe deeply:** Take a few deep breaths to help you relax.

3. **Visualise a peaceful scene:** Imagine yourself in a peaceful, relaxing place. This could be a beach, a forest, a mountain, or any place where you feel calm and safe.
4. **Engage your senses:** Use your imagination to engage all your senses. What do you see, hear, smell, and feel in this place? Immerse yourself fully in the experience.
5. **Stay in the scene:** Spend a few minutes enjoying this peaceful scene. Whenever your mind starts to wander, gently bring it back to the visualisation.
6. **Return to the present:** When you're ready to finish, slowly bring your awareness back to the present moment. Take a few deep breaths and open your eyes.

Finding "Me Time"

In our crucial roles, I know how tricky it can be to carve out time for ourselves amidst the whirlwind of daily responsibilities. Some days, getting a moment alone feels like trying to sneak out of a toddler's room without stepping on a squeaky toy! But honestly, implementing a few simple strategies can help us create those precious pockets of time for self-care. This little investment in ourselves can lead to improved well-being and a more balanced, joyful life. Let's embrace these moments together—before someone yells, "Muuum!" again!

Schedule It In

Scheduling time for yourself is crucial because it prioritises self-care in the same way you prioritise other commitments. Consider using a digital calendar or planner to block out specific times for activities that recharge you. This could be as simple as a 10-minute daily meditation or a 30-minute weekly hobby session. By treating these moments as non-negotiable appointments, you increase the likelihood of actually taking this time for yourself.

Wake Up Earlier

Waking up earlier can provide a peaceful start to your day before the hustle and bustle begins. This early time can be used for activities that might be difficult to fit in during the day, such as a short workout, reading, or planning your day. The quiet of the early morning can help set a positive tone for the rest of the day and give you a head start on your personal goals.

Utilise Nap Time

Nap time is a golden opportunity for self-care, but it can be tempting to use this time to catch up on household chores or work tasks. Instead, try to reserve part of nap time for activities that rejuvenate you. You might use this time to read a book, take a power nap yourself, or engage in a hobby. If possible, create a relaxing environment during nap time to fully enjoy this break.

Create a Relaxing Evening Routine

A calming evening routine can help you transition from the day's responsibilities to a restful night's sleep. Consider incorporating activities that promote relaxation, such as a warm bath with essential oils, gentle stretching or mindfulness exercises. Establishing this routine not only helps you unwind but also signals to your body that it's time to wind down, improving your overall sleep quality.

Delegate Tasks

Delegating tasks can significantly reduce your workload and stress levels. Discuss with your partner or family members how tasks can be shared or outsourced. This might include household chores, meal preparation, or even childcare. If possible, hiring help for specific tasks, like cleaning or grocery shopping, can also free up valuable time for you. Effective delegation not only provides you with more personal time but also involves others in maintaining the household.

Combine Activities

Combining self-care with other daily activities can maximise your time and efficiency. For instance, you could listen to a motivational podcast or soothing music while doing household chores. Engaging in mindfulness exercises during your commute or cooking can also be beneficial. By integrating self-care into routine activities, you make it easier to maintain these practices regularly without feeling overwhelmed.

The Role of Meditation In My Coaching Practice

In my coaching practice, I emphasise the importance of meditation for my clients. I encourage them to meditate for at least 10 minutes before going to bed as a way to unwind and relax. This practice helps to clear the mind, reduce stress, and improve sleep quality. Here are some specific benefits of incorporating meditation into your evening routine:

Improved Sleep Quality

Meditation before bed helps to relax the mind and body, making it easier to fall asleep and stay asleep. By calming the mind and reducing the activity of the nervous system, meditation promotes a deeper, more restful sleep.

Stress Reduction

The practice of meditation helps to reduce stress levels by promoting relaxation and lowering cortisol levels. This can lead to a more peaceful and restful night's sleep.

Mental Clarity

Meditation helps to clear the mind of the day's worries and distractions, allowing you to enter a state of mental clarity and calm. This can improve the quality of your sleep and leave you feeling more refreshed in the morning.

The Science Behind Meditation

Meditation, a practice rooted in ancient traditions, has gained widespread popularity in modern times, not just for its spiritual benefits but for its profound impact on mental and physical health. Science has increasingly supported the benefits of meditation, revealing how this simple practice can lead to significant changes in the brain, hormone levels, and overall well-being. For mums on the go, understanding these benefits can provide the motivation to integrate meditation into their daily routines, despite the challenges of a hectic lifestyle.

Brain Changes

One of the most compelling aspects of meditation is its ability to physically alter the brain's structure. Numerous studies using advanced neuroimaging techniques have shown that regular meditation can lead to measurable changes in various parts of the brain. For instance, meditation has been found to increase grey matter density in regions associated with learning, memory, and emotional regulation, such as the hippocampus. This suggests that meditation not only helps with stress management but can also enhance cognitive functions, making it easier to navigate the complexities of everyday life.

Additionally, meditation has a significant impact on the amygdala, a small almond-shaped structure in the brain responsible for the fight-or-flight response. The amygdala plays a crucial role in how we process fear and anxiety. Research has shown that regular meditation can reduce the size and activity of the amygdala, leading to lower levels of stress and anxiety. This is particularly beneficial for busy mums who often juggle multiple responsibilities and can easily become overwhelmed. By regularly engaging in meditation, mums can cultivate a calmer, more resilient mindset, better equipped to handle the challenges of parenting and daily life.

Another fascinating finding is the increased connectivity between the prefrontal cortex and other regions of the brain. The prefrontal cortex is involved in decision-making, attention, and self-regulation. Enhanced connectivity in this area due to meditation can lead to improved focus, better decision-making, and greater emotional regulation.

These changes make it easier to stay present, make thoughtful choices, and respond to stressful situations with greater clarity and calmness.

Hormonal Benefits

Beyond the brain, meditation also profoundly impacts the body's hormonal balance. One of the primary ways it does this is by reducing levels of cortisol, the body's main stress hormone. Cortisol is essential for various bodily functions, but when produced in excess due to chronic stress, it can lead to numerous health issues, including impaired immune function, weight gain, and difficulty sleeping. By lowering cortisol levels, meditation helps to mitigate these negative effects, promoting a more balanced and healthy physiological state.

In addition to reducing cortisol, meditation can also boost the production of feel-good neurotransmitters like serotonin and dopamine. These chemicals play a crucial role in regulating mood, sleep, and overall well-being. Serotonin, often referred to as the "happiness hormone," is associated with feelings of well-being and happiness. Dopamine, on the other hand, is linked to pleasure, reward, and motivation. By increasing the levels of these neurotransmitters, meditation can enhance mood, improve sleep quality, and provide a sense of inner peace and contentment.

For mothers like us these hormonal benefits can be transformative. The demands of parenting can lead to chronic stress and exhaustion, but by incorporating even short meditation sessions into their day, we can help regulate our mood, boost energy levels, and improve our overall sense of well-being. This not only benefits us but also has a positive ripple effect on our children and family life.

Given the science-backed benefits of meditation, it's clear that this practice is worth the effort. However, the challenge for many of us is finding the time and energy to meditate amidst a demanding schedule. Here are some practical tips to help you integrate meditation into your daily life, ensuring that you can reap the benefits without feeling overwhelmed.

Set Realistic Expectations

One of the most important things to remember is that meditation doesn't have to be a lengthy or complex process. The key is consistency. By setting realistic expectations, you'll be more likely to stick with your practice and see the long-term benefits.

Make It a Habit

Consistency is crucial when it comes to meditation. To establish a regular practice, try to meditate at the same time each day. This could be first thing in the morning, during a lunch break, or before bed—whatever time works best for you. By making meditation a non-negotiable part of your daily routine, it becomes a habit, just like brushing your teeth or having your morning coffee. Over time, you'll find that this regular practice helps you navigate the ups and downs of life with greater ease and resilience.

Use Technology

In today's digital age, there are countless resources available to help you get started with meditation. Apps like Headspace, Calm, and Insight Timer offer guided meditations, meditation courses, and tools to track your progress. These apps can be particularly helpful for beginners, providing structure and support as you develop your practice. They also offer a variety of meditation styles and lengths, allowing you to choose what works best for you. By leveraging technology, you can make meditation more accessible and tailored to your needs.

Involve Your Children

For my mothers with young children, finding time alone to meditate can be challenging. However, instead of seeing this as a barrier, consider involving your children in your meditation practice. There are many kid-friendly meditation resources available that can help teach mindfulness to children in a fun and engaging way. Meditating together can be a wonderful bonding experience and can help establish healthy habits for your children. By making meditation a family activity, you can foster a calm and mindful atmosphere at home, benefiting everyone.

Be Flexible

Life with children is inherently unpredictable, and there will be days when your meditation plans don't go as expected. It's important to be flexible and not too hard on yourself if you miss a session or if your meditation time gets interrupted. Remember that the goal is to make meditation a regular part of your routine, but it doesn't have to be perfect. If you miss a session, simply try to fit it in when you can, even if it's just a quick few minutes of deep breathing. By being kind to yourself and adaptable, you'll find it easier to maintain your meditation practice in the long run.

Three-Minute Breathing Space

This quick meditation exercise is perfect for those moments when you need a brief mental break:

1. **Find a quiet space:** Sit or stand in a comfortable position.
2. **Close your eyes and breathe deeply:** Take a few deep breaths to help you relax.
3. **Focus on your breath:** Bring your attention to your breath and notice the sensation of the air entering and leaving your nostrils.
4. **Expand your awareness:** Gradually expand your awareness to include your body and any sensations you're experiencing.
5. **Return to your breath:** After a few minutes, bring your focus back to your breath and then slowly open your eyes.

Five Senses Exercise

This mindfulness exercise helps ground you in the present moment by focusing on your five senses:

- **Find a quiet space:** Sit or stand in a comfortable position.
- **Close your eyes and breathe deeply:** Take a few deep breaths to help you relax.
- **Notice five things you can see:** Open your eyes and observe your surroundings. Take note of five things you can see.
- **Notice four things you can hear:** Close your eyes and focus on the sounds around you. Identify four things you can hear.
- **Notice three things you can feel:** Pay attention to the physical sensations in your body. Notice three things you can feel.
- **Notice two things you can smell:** Focus on your sense of smell and identify two scents.
- **Notice one thing you can taste:** Pay attention to your sense of taste and notice any lingering flavours in your mouth.
- **Take a deep breath:** Finish the exercise with a deep breath and slowly open your eyes.

Key Takeaways

Meditation is truly a game-changer for our mental and emotional well-being. By weaving a bit of meditation into our busy lives, we can unlock a treasure trove of benefits—like lower stress levels, sharper focus, and even better sleep. I know how tough it can be to find those few extra minutes in our hectic schedules as busy mums, but trust me, even a short daily practice can make a world of difference. Let's prioritise self-care together and carve out that time for ourselves, so we can embrace the amazing, transformative benefits of meditation. You deserve it!

Chapter 2: Kick the Mundane Daily Routine

Let's take a moment to break free from the daily grind and inject some much-needed fun, creativity, and fulfilment into our lives. Yes, routines are essential, they help us keep things running smoothly, especially with all the responsibilities we juggle. But let's be honest, sometimes they can feel like a trap, leaving us drained and stuck in autopilot. The trick is figuring out the difference between being busy and being truly productive. We've all been there, caught in a whirlwind of tasks that leave us feeling wiped out but somehow unaccomplished. Real productivity, though, fills us up. It gives us a sense of satisfaction, like we've moved the needle, even just a little.

In this chapter, we're going to figure out whether you're truly productive or simply stuck in a cycle of endless to-dos. And more importantly, I'll share some practical steps to help you break free from the mundane routine. You deserve to feel fulfilled and valued in your daily life, not just like a taskmaster ticking boxes. When we go through the motions, completing tasks just to get them done, we often miss out on the simple joy that comes from doing something meaningful.

I know it's easy to fall into a rut when everything starts to feel like the same old routine—like you're living a real-life version of "Groundhog Day." If that resonates, then it's time to stir things up! Let's find ways to add a little spice, a little excitement to your everyday life. Imagine waking up excited, with a smile, because today isn't just another day of getting through the chores. Instead, it's full of moments that bring you joy and make you feel alive. Sounds amazing, right? Let's turn that vision into your new reality!

Reflecting on Past Freedom

Frankly, with our demands of motherhood & work deadlines, "free time" sounds like a myth, right? But let's take a real moment here to those rare, magical moments where you actually felt a little bit of freedom—like when the kids miraculously slept in, and you got to enjoy your coffee while it was still hot (pure bliss!), or when you snuck in a bath without someone knocking on the door asking for snacks. Those moments might seem tiny, but they're the ones that fill you up and make you feel like yourself again, even if just for a bit.

I remember one beach day with my son & his cousins—usually, it's all about keeping them from eating sand or losing a flip-flop. But this time, they were fully occupied with their sandcastles, and I actually got to sit down, close my eyes, and just breathe in that salty ocean air. It wasn't a spa day, but for a few minutes, it was just me and the sound of the waves—heavenly. Another time, I signed up for a painter's workshop (not exactly something I do regularly), but stepping away from my normal routine and having a laugh with people I am meeting for the first time—did wonders for my mood and reminded me how much I love getting creative.

Now it's your turn—grab a notebook (or let's be real, jot it down on your phone between school pickups) and think about a few moments like that. When did you last feel calm, free, or like the fun version of yourself? Maybe it was catching up with friends, sneaking in a solo walk, or just having a rare laugh-out-loud moment. Reflect on what made those moments feel so good and how they recharged you. Was it the quiet? The company? The break from the usual chaos?

This isn't about wishing you were back in some golden age of more "me time." It's about realising that even in the middle of the mum-life madness, you can carve out little moments like those to recharge. You've done it before—now, let's figure out how to sprinkle more of that magic into the everyday hustle!

Creating a Fulfilling Schedule

Once you've identified activities that make you feel free and happy, it's time to integrate them into your current routine. This isn't about adding more to your plate; it's about replacing unproductive or mundane tasks with activities that bring fulfilment. Let's craft a schedule that includes these joyful activities.

Imagine your week as a canvas, and you have the brush to paint it with vibrant, fulfilling colours. Start by identifying the activities from your past that brought you joy. Whether it's dancing, painting, hiking, or simply reading a book, make a list of these activities and think about how you can incorporate them into your current life.

For instance, instead of your regular evening workout, have a dance party in your living room. Blast your favourite tunes and dance like nobody's watching. If you love painting, dedicate an hour each week to create art. These small changes can lead to significant improvements in mental well-being.

Look at your current schedule and identify pockets of time that can be dedicated to these activities. This might involve waking up earlier, using lunch breaks creatively, or reallocating time from less fulfilling tasks. The idea is to replace the mundane with the magical, the boring with the beautiful.

Monday Madness: Dance Party

Transform your Monday evenings into a dance party. Clear some space in your living room, turn up your favourite playlist, and dance like nobody's watching. Feel the music, let go of your inhibitions, and enjoy the pure joy of movement. Dancing is not only a fantastic workout but also a great way to release stress and boost your mood. Plus, it's a fun activity that the whole family can join in on. Imagine the joy of starting your week with a burst of energy, shaking off the Monday blues with a freestyle dance session. You don't need any fancy equipment or professional skills, just your favourite music and the willingness to let loose. The beauty of dancing is that it engages both your body and mind, lifting your spirits and setting a positive tone for the rest of the week.

Tuesday Tranquillity: Creative Hour

Dedicate an hour on Tuesdays to a creative activity you love. Whether it's painting, writing, knitting, or building a Lego castle, let your imagination run wild. Creativity is a powerful way to express yourself and can bring immense satisfaction. Set up a cosy corner with your art supplies, play some soothing music, and immerse yourself in the joy of creating something beautiful. Creativity is not just about making art; it's about exploring your inner world and expressing it in a tangible form. When you engage in creative activities, you tap into a different part of your brain, fostering innovation and problem-solving skills. It's a therapeutic process that can reduce stress, improve mood, and enhance cognitive function.

Wednesday Wonder: Explore Something New

Make Wednesdays your day for discovery. Try a new recipe, visit a new part of town, or take an online class. Exploring something new can be exhilarating and break the monotony of your routine. For example, if you've always wanted to learn how to cook Italian cuisine, find a recipe online and try it out. Or, if there's a museum you've never visited, plan a visit and spend a few hours exploring. The goal is to step out of your comfort zone and experience something different. Trying new things keeps life exciting and fresh. It stimulates your brain, builds confidence, and can even spark new interests and hobbies. Whether it's learning a new language, taking up a new sport, or simply visiting a different neighbourhood, the experience of something new can provide a welcome break from the ordinary.

Thursday Thrills: Outdoor Adventure

Thursdays are perfect for outdoor adventures. Go for a hike, bike ride, or simply walk in a nearby park. Reconnecting with nature can have a profound impact on your mental and physical well-being. Take in the fresh air, listen to the sounds of nature, and let the beauty of the outdoors rejuvenate you. If you have children, make it a family outing and explore new trails together. Spending time in nature has numerous benefits, including reducing stress, improving mood, and enhancing physical health. Nature walks can be meditative, allowing you to clear your mind and focus on the present moment. Plus, it's a great way to stay active and enjoy quality time with your family.

Friday Fun: Social Hour

End the week with some social fun. Meet up with friends, join a local event, or have a family game night. Social connections are crucial for well-being, and spending time with loved ones can be incredibly fulfilling. Plan a dinner with friends, attend a community event, or host a game night at home. Laughter and camaraderie are great ways to de-stress and end the week on a high note. Human connections are essential for emotional health. Socialising can boost your mood, provide support during tough times, and even improve cognitive function. Whether you're catching up with old friends or making new ones, the joy of shared experiences can significantly enhance your quality of life.

The Power of Small Changes

Making small changes to your daily routine can significantly boost your overall well-being, especially for us mums juggling countless responsibilities. Life rarely goes as planned—kids get sick, schedules shift, and unexpected events arise. Embracing change can help you navigate these challenges with grace.

Consider starting your day with a simple morning ritual. Instead of rushing out the door, take a moment to reflect on three things you're grateful for. It could be as simple as enjoying your favourite coffee, appreciating a moment of quiet before the chaos begins, or feeling grateful for your children's laughter. This practice can shift your focus and help you find positivity amid the morning rush.

You might also find it helpful to incorporate quick stretches or a few deep breaths while waiting for your morning coffee to brew. It doesn't have to be a full yoga routine—just a minute or two to wake up your body and clear your mind before tackling the day's to-do list.

During your busy day, remember to use small pockets of time effectively. For example, if you have a few minutes between tasks, try the Pomodoro Technique: work intensely for 25 minutes, then take a 5-minute break to grab a snack or check in with your little ones. This can help you stay focused while also keeping you refreshed.

Keeping your workspace organised is another simple but impactful change. A tidy area can help you concentrate better and reduce stress. And don't forget to sneak in short breaks—whether it's a brisk walk around the house, or a few moments of mindful breathing. These pauses can recharge your energy and improve your focus.

At the end of the day, wind down with calming activities that bring you joy. A leisurely walk with your partner or children after dinner can help you unwind and reflect on the day's highlights. Try to turn off screens at least an hour before bed to create a peaceful environment for sleep. Spending just 10 minutes journaling about your day can also ease your mind and prepare you for restful sleep.

These small adjustments can create a ripple effect, enhancing your mental well-being and overall quality of life, allowing you to tackle each day with renewed energy and a positive mindset.

Trying Something New

Stepping out of your comfort zone and trying new activities can be incredibly rewarding, especially for mums like us who often find ourselves stuck in a routine. Life can feel predictable, with the same tasks repeating day in and day out. However, embracing change can not only add excitement but also foster personal growth and new connections.

Think about how refreshing it can be to sign up for a local cooking class where you can learn to make healthy meals that your family will love. Not only does this give you a break from your usual dinner prep, but it also allows you to meet other parents in your community who share your interests. Or perhaps you've always wanted to try yoga, but with school runs and endless errands, it feels challenging. Many local studios offer introductory classes or mum-and-baby sessions, making it easier to get started.

Consider joining a book club or a walking group through platforms like Meetup. These are excellent ways to connect with other mums while engaging in something you enjoy. You could even organise a casual "mums' night out" to explore a new restaurant or attend a community event together.

Even something as simple as hosting a game night at home can provide a welcome change. Invite a few friends over, prepare some snacks, and enjoy an evening of laughter and connection. Trying new activities doesn't always have to involve a big-time commitment or financial investment. Sometimes, it's just about being open to new experiences that fit into your busy life.

At the beginning of the year, I committed to running a half marathon to raise funds for my son's school. While I exercise regularly, running isn't my forte, so I knew I would need to train extensively for this challenge. As a single parent, like many others, I have limited free time outside of work and parenting responsibilities. To make it work, I decided to combine my training with quality time spent with my son; he would ride his scooter or bike while I jogged alongside him. This approach was highly effective, allowing us to converse and appreciate nature together during our outings. We maintained this new routine for three months, and both of us found it enjoyable.

The key is to choose activities that excite you and align with your values. Whether it's discovering a new hobby, attending a local event, or just meeting new people, these small changes can have a significant impact on your well-being, adding joy and variety to your routine while helping you build a supportive network of friends.

Free Events and Social Connections

Exploring new activities doesn't have to break the bank, especially for single parents looking for ways to inject some fun into their routine. Websites like Eventbrite and Meetup offer a wealth of free events and opportunities to connect with others in your local community.

Eventbrite is a fantastic resource for finding free workshops, community gatherings, and local events. Just filter for free activities in your area and browse categories like health, arts, or family-friendly outings. For example, you might find a free gardening workshop where you can learn how to create a small vegetable patch at home, perfect for involving the children and teaching them about healthy eating. Bringing a friend along can make it even more enjoyable and provide a bit of accountability.

Meetup is all about bringing people together based on shared interests. Sign up, join groups that reflect your hobbies, and RSVP to events that pique your interest. Imagine joining a local book club where you can discuss the latest novels while enjoying a cup of coffee. It's a great way to take a break from the daily grind and connect with like-minded mums who also love reading.

For instance, one mum I know - always juggling her demanding job & home- asked for a sabbatical from work and was granted it. She discovered a local hiking group on Meetup. Not only did she get to explore beautiful trails she never knew existed, but she also forged friendships with other mothers who understood her daily challenges.

These experiences not only enrich your life but also add a sense of adventure and community to your routine. By stepping out of your comfort zone and embracing new opportunities, you can break free from monotony and enjoy the company of others, all while keeping costs down.

Evaluating Current Activities

To determine if your daily routine is productive or just busy, take a moment to step back and evaluate your schedule, especially if it feels like there is no off button until bedtime. Juggling work, family, and household responsibilities can leave little time for what truly matters. Ask yourself: Am I getting the most out of my day? Do I feel valued and fulfilled? Reflecting on these questions can help you identify whether your activities align with your personal goals and values.

For example, if you find you're spending hours cleaning the house but feeling exhausted and unappreciated, it might be time to rethink how you approach those tasks. Instead of trying to do it all, consider delegating some chores to your children, partner or even enlisting help from a friend. You could create a family chore chart that not only lightens your load but also teaches your children about responsibility. This way, you can spend more time enjoying activities together, like baking cookies or playing games.

Also, think about whether your current commitments bring you joy. If you find yourself overwhelmed with obligations, such as organising the school bake sale or volunteering for every event, it may be time to set some boundaries. It's okay to say no to tasks that drain your energy or don't align with your priorities.

Instead, prioritise activities that ignite your passion, whether it's joining a local art class, starting a book club, or simply carving out time to catch up with friends over coffee. These pursuits not only showcase your strengths but also nourish your spirit. By making adjustments based on your reflections, you can create a schedule that's not just busy, but truly fulfilling, allowing you to feel valued and accomplished in your daily life.

Supporting Research

Research supports the idea that learning new things and making small changes can significantly improve mental well-being. According to the NHS, engaging in new activities and learning can boost self-esteem, build a sense of purpose, and improve social connections. These factors contribute to overall mental health and happiness. Here's the title to their findings: Five Steps to Mental Wellbeing.

Practical Exercises and Tip

To help you identify fulfilling activities and integrate them into your routine, here are some practical exercises and tips: Reflective Journaling: Use journaling as a way to reflect on your day and identify areas for improvement. Write about your daily experiences, focusing on what went well and what could be improved. Set short-term and long-term goals for yourself and track your progress in your journal. Incorporate gratitude journaling to cultivate a positive mindset.

Mindful Reflection: Practise mindful reflection by taking a few minutes each day to sit quietly and reflect on your thoughts and feelings. Find a quiet space, close your eyes, and take a few deep breaths to centre yourself. Think about your day and consider what brought you joy, what challenges you faced, and how you can improve.

Integrate New and Old Activities: Identify activities from your past that brought you joy and find ways to incorporate them into your current routine. Try new activities that excite you and align with your values and interests. Use resources like Eventbrite and Meetup to find free events and opportunities to meet new people.

Make Small, Impactful Changes: Incorporate minor adjustments to your routine to break the monotony. Start your day with a positive morning ritual, take short breaks during work to stretch or walk, and end the day with a relaxing activity like reading or meditating. These small changes can lead to significant improvements in mental well-being.

Embracing Change: Overcoming the fear of the unknown

Change is one of the few constants in life, yet it is something that many people struggle to embrace. The fear of the unknown often holds us back, trapping us in routines and behaviours that no longer serve us. However, embracing change is crucial for personal growth and fulfilment. This section will explore the nature of change, why it is essential, and how to overcome the fear that accompanies it.

The Nature of Change

Change is inevitable. It can be as simple as a change in the weather or as complex as a significant life transition, like moving to a new city or changing careers. While some changes are welcomed and even eagerly anticipated, others can be frightening and overwhelming. Regardless of its form, change forces us to adapt, learn, and grow. Without change, life would be stagnant and predictable, leaving little room for personal development or new experiences.

Change challenges our comfort zones. When we become accustomed to a certain way of living, thinking, or working, it creates a sense of security. This comfort zone is familiar, and even if it is not entirely satisfying, it is predictable. Stepping out of this zone requires courage, as it involves venturing into the unknown—a place where outcomes are uncertain and risks are higher.

The Fear of The Unknown

The fear of the unknown is a natural human response. It stems from our survival instincts, which are designed to protect us from potential threats. When faced with uncertainty, the brain's amygdala, responsible for the fight-or-flight response, triggers feelings of anxiety and apprehension. This response was useful in ancient times when our ancestors needed to be wary of dangers in their environment. However, in modern life, this fear can prevent us from making changes that could improve our well-being. Fear of the unknown manifests in various ways. It might show up as procrastination, where we delay making decisions or taking actions because we are unsure of the outcome. It can also appear as self-doubt, where we question our abilities and fear failure. In some cases, it leads to clinging to the status quo, even when it no longer serves us, simply because the alternative is unknown.

Why Change is Essential

Despite the discomfort it brings, change is essential for growth. Without change, we would remain stagnant, never learning, evolving, or reaching our full potential. Embracing change allows us to discover new opportunities, develop new skills, and experience life in a more fulfilling way. Change often leads to new opportunities. Whether it's a career change, a new relationship, or a move to a different location, embracing change opens doors to possibilities that would have remained closed if we had stayed in our comfort zones. These opportunities can lead to personal growth, greater happiness, and a more enriched life. Additionally, change is a powerful teacher. It challenges us to develop resilience, adaptability, and problem-solving skills. When we face change, we learn to navigate uncertainty, manage stress, and find creative solutions to new challenges. These skills are not only valuable in the context of the specific change but also in other areas of life, making us more capable and confident individuals.

At the start of this book, I shared that you're not alone in your feelings and that "a problem shared is a problem halved." What I hadn't yet discussed was my journey overcoming "mum guilt," which lingered for a year after I returned to work. I remember the daily routine—leaving my son at nursery, rushing through the workday, returning home for bedtime, only to repeat it all the next day. I felt constantly short on time and found myself eagerly awaiting the weekends. While I loved my job, I felt unfulfilled as a parent to my only child, so I decided to seek roles that allowed me to work from home. This change eliminated lengthy commutes and provided the flexibility that has since become known as work-life balance.

While working from home may not be for everyone, we each deserve the best quality of life we can create. For some, that might mean considering part-time or flexible work options. Many job sites now cater specifically to parents returning to the workforce, including workingmums.co.uk, mummyjobs.co.uk, momprojects.com, and wherewomenwork.com.

Overcoming the Fear of Change

While the fear of change is natural, it doesn't have to control our lives. There are strategies we can use to overcome this fear and embrace change more confidently.

1. Acknowledge Your Fear
2. Educate Yourself
3. Break It Down
4. Visualise Success
5. Seek Support
6. Practice Resilience
7. Focus on the Benefits

The first step in overcoming the fear of change is to acknowledge it. Recognise that fear is a natural response to uncertainty and that it is okay to feel apprehensive. By acknowledging your fear, you can begin to address it rather than letting it paralyse you. Often, the fear of the unknown stems from a lack of information. The more you know about the change you are facing, the less intimidating it will seem. Research, ask questions, and gather as much information as possible. This knowledge will help you feel more prepared and confident in dealing with the change. Big changes can be overwhelming, but breaking them down into smaller, manageable steps can make them more approachable.

Focus on one step at a time, rather than the entire change. This approach reduces the feeling of being overwhelmed and allows you to make progress at your own pace. Visualisation is a powerful tool for overcoming fear. Imagine yourself successfully navigating the change and experiencing the positive outcomes it will bring. This mental rehearsal can help build confidence and reduce anxiety. You don't have to face change alone. Reach out to friends, family, or a mentor for support. Talking about your fears and concerns with someone you trust can provide reassurance and help you gain perspective. Instead of dwelling on the potential risks or negative aspects of change, focus on the benefits it can bring. Remind yourself of the opportunities for growth, the new experiences, and the positive outcomes that can result from embracing change. Building resilience is key to handling change effectively. Resilience involves developing a positive attitude, staying flexible, and learning to bounce back from setbacks. By cultivating resilience, you can face change with greater confidence and adaptability.

Mindful Living: Being Present in the Moment

In our fast-paced world, it's easy to get caught up in the whirlwind of daily tasks and responsibilities. We often find ourselves rushing from one activity to the next, barely taking a moment to breathe, let alone reflect on our actions. This constant busyness can lead to a life that feels unfulfilling and disconnected. Mindful living offers a solution by encouraging us to slow down, be present in the moment, and fully engage with our experiences.

The Concept of Mindfulness

Mindfulness is the practice of being fully present and aware of the current moment, without judgement or distraction. It involves paying attention to your thoughts, feelings, and surroundings with a sense of curiosity and openness. Mindfulness is not about emptying your mind or avoiding thoughts; rather, it's about observing your thoughts and feelings without getting caught up in them.

The roots of mindfulness can be traced back to ancient meditation practices, particularly in Buddhism. However, in recent years, mindfulness has gained popularity in the West as a secular practice that can benefit anyone, regardless of their religious or spiritual beliefs. Research has shown that mindfulness can improve mental health, reduce stress, and enhance overall well-being.

The Benefits of Mindful Living

Mindful living offers numerous benefits, both for our mental and physical health. By being present in the moment, we can reduce stress, improve focus, and enhance our relationships with others.

Reduced Stress: One of the most significant benefits of mindfulness is its ability to reduce stress. When we are mindful, we are less likely to get caught up in worries about the future or regrets about the past. Instead, we focus on the present moment, which helps to calm the mind and reduce feelings of anxiety.

Mindfulness helps improve focus and concentration. By training our minds to stay present, we can reduce distractions and improve our ability to concentrate on tasks. This enhanced focus can lead to greater productivity and a sense of accomplishment.

Mindful living can also improve our relationships with others. When we are fully present with the people around us, we listen more deeply, communicate more effectively, and respond with greater empathy and understanding. This leads to stronger, more meaningful connections. Mindfulness helps us become more aware of our emotions

and how they influence our thoughts and behaviours. By observing our emotions without judgement, we can learn to respond to situations more calmly and thoughtfully, rather than reacting impulsively. Mindfulness has been linked to increased feelings of happiness and contentment. By focusing on the present moment, we can appreciate the simple pleasures of life, such as the warmth of the sun on our skin or the taste of a delicious meal. This heightened awareness of the present moment can lead to a greater sense of gratitude and overall happiness.

How to Practise Mindful Living

Mindful living is a practice that can be incorporated into various aspects of your life. Here are some practical ways to bring mindfulness into your daily routine:

- **Mindful Breathing:** One of the simplest ways to practise mindfulness is through mindful breathing. Take a few minutes each day to focus on your breath. Notice the sensation of the air entering and leaving your body. If your mind starts to wander, gently bring your attention back to your breath. This practice can be done anywhere, at any time, and is a powerful way to anchor yourself in the present moment.
- **Mindful Eating:** Eating mindfully involves paying full attention to the experience of eating. This means savouring each bite, noticing the Flavors, textures, and aromas of your food, and being aware of the sensations in your body as you eat. Mindful eating can help you develop a healthier relationship with food, as it encourages you to eat with intention and awareness, rather than out of habit or emotion.
- **Mindful Movement:** Incorporate mindfulness into your physical activities, such as walking, yoga, or exercise. Focus on the sensations in your body as you move, the rhythm of your breath, and the environment around you. Mindful movement helps you connect with your body and brings a sense of calm and focus to your physical activities.
- **Mindful Listening:** Practise mindful listening when interacting with others. Give the person your full attention, without interrupting or planning your response while they are speaking. Notice their tone of voice, body language, and the emotions behind their words. Mindful listening fosters deeper connections and more meaningful conversations.
- **Mindful Reflection:** Set aside time each day for mindful reflection. This could be through journaling, meditation, or simply sitting quietly and reflecting on your day

Key Takeaways

As we journey through life, change is an inevitable companion, and how we respond to it shapes our growth and fulfilment. The fear of the unknown can hold us back, but by embracing change with courage and resilience, we unlock opportunities for personal development and a richer life experience. The strategies discussed—acknowledging our fears, breaking down challenges into manageable steps, seeking support, and focusing on the positive outcomes—equip us to face change with confidence. Equally important is the practice of mindfulness, which anchors us in the present moment, allowing us to fully engage with our experiences and appreciate the richness of life as it unfolds. By incorporating mindfulness into our daily routines—through mindful breathing, eating, movement, listening, and reflection—we enhance our mental and emotional well-being, reduce stress, and foster deeper connections with ourselves and others. Together, the principles of embracing change and living mindfully empower us to navigate life's transitions with grace and intentionality. They remind us that while we cannot always control the changes that come our way, we can control how we respond to them. By choosing to embrace change and cultivate mindfulness, we open ourselves to a life of greater purpose, connection, and fulfilment. As you continue on your journey, remember that life is not a series of isolated events but a continuous flow of moments, each offering its own lessons and opportunities. Embrace the changes that come your way, stay present in the moment, and trust that by doing so, you are crafting a life that is truly your own—a life lived fully and authentically.

References

Eventbrite, Free Events. Retrieved from Eventbrite

Meetup, Find Your People. Retrieved from Meetup

NHS, Five Steps to Mental Wellbeing. Retrieved from NHS

Chapter 3: Promoting Health and Wellness During Menopause

Menopause is a significant transition in a woman's life, marked by the cessation of menstruation and a host of physical, emotional, and psychological changes. This natural process typically occurs in women between the ages of 45 and 55, though the timing can vary widely. As the body adjusts to lower levels of oestrogen and other hormones, women may experience symptoms such as hot flashes, night sweats, mood swings, and weight gain. These changes can be challenging, but adopting a proactive approach to health and wellness can help women navigate this phase more smoothly.

In this chapter we explore the critical role that physical activity, social engagement, and a balanced diet play in managing menopausal symptoms. By staying active, connecting with supportive communities, and making informed dietary choices, we can significantly improve our quality of life during and after menopause. Social media platforms like Facebook, Instagram, and Tiktok provide accessible ways to join or create active groups aimed at women. In particular some of my friends have joined walking groups through these platforms, offering not only physical benefits but also emotional support. Additionally, the chapter will delve into the scientific evidence supporting the benefits of physical activity and a balanced diet during menopause, providing practical tips and guidance for integrating these into daily life.

The Importance of Physical Activity During Menopause

Staying active is one of the best gifts you can give yourself, especially as we navigate through life's different stages, including menopause. With our busy schedules, we often put everyone else's needs ahead of our own, but making time for physical activity is essential for keeping our health in check—both physically and emotionally. During menopause, when things like weight gain, mood swings, and hot flashes can pop up, regular exercise can be a real game changer.

Let's be real, the body changes we go through during this time—like a slower metabolism and reduced muscle tone—can make it tougher to stay in shape. But that doesn't mean it's impossible! In fact, staying active can help combat these shifts by boosting your metabolism, toning your muscles, and keeping you feeling more energised and fit. Plus, exercise is one of the best ways to clear your mind, reduce stress, and even balance those unpredictable mood swings.

You don't need to become a gym warrior to feel the benefits. Whether it's a brisk walk while the children are at school, dancing around the house while doing chores, or joining a local class to stretch and unwind—every bit counts. The key is finding something you enjoy, that fits into your schedule, and that makes you feel good. It's not about perfection, but about giving yourself the care and attention you deserve as you navigate this important phase of life.

Impact of Physical Activity

One of the most well-documented benefits of physical activity during menopause is its ability to improve mood and reduce stress. The hormonal fluctuations that occur during menopause can lead to mood swings, anxiety, and even depression. Exercise, particularly aerobic activities like walking, jogging, or cycling, triggers the release of endorphins—often referred to as "feel-good" hormones—which can help alleviate these symptoms. Moreover, regular physical activity has been shown to reduce the severity and frequency of hot flashes, one of the most common and bothersome symptoms of menopause.

According to the NHS Inform, engaging in regular physical activity can make a substantial difference in managing menopausal symptoms. The article highlights that staying active not only helps with weight management but also improves cardiovascular health, strengthens bones, and enhances mental well-being. Weight-bearing exercises, such as walking or resistance training, are particularly beneficial as they help maintain bone density, reducing the risk of osteoporosis, a condition that becomes more prevalent after menopause due to decreased estrogen levels.

Another significant benefit of physical activity during menopause is the positive impact on sleep quality. Many women experience sleep disturbances during menopause, such as insomnia or waking up frequently during the night. Exercise can help regulate the sleep-wake cycle, making it easier to fall asleep and stay asleep. Additionally, being physically active during the day can help reduce feelings of fatigue and improve energy levels, making it easier to engage in daily activities and maintain a positive outlook.

Mental Health Benefits

Physical activity isn't just good for our bodies—it's also key to maintaining a balanced mood, which can make all the difference in how we interact with others. Exercise naturally releases endorphins, lifting our mood and reducing stress, which helps me manage those moments when my patience is tested—something I know many of us experience, especially with our children. By staying active, I find I'm better able to approach situations with a calm mindset, making me more present and engaged with my son and others, rather than getting easily frustrated. Even simple activities like walking or yoga have a powerful effect, allowing me to enjoy family time with greater patience and positivity.

The key is consistency—regular, moderate exercise is more beneficial than sporadic, intense workouts. Women should aim for at least 150 minutes of moderate-intensity aerobic activity per week, combined with muscle-strengthening activities on two or more days a week.

Encouraging Social Interaction Through Group Activities

One of the most effective ways to stay motivated and consistent with physical activity during menopause is to join a community or group that shares similar goals. Women's walking groups, as mentioned earlier, have gained popularity as a supportive and social way to stay active. These groups not only provide the physical benefits of regular exercise but also unconsciously provide emotional and psychological support, which is crucial during the menopausal transition.

Social Media Platforms

In today's digital age, social media platforms like Facebook and Instagram have become powerful tools for connecting people with shared interests. Numerous women's groups have been established on these platforms, offering a convenient way to find local activities, share experiences, and stay motivated. These groups often provide a sense of camaraderie, as members can relate to each other's experiences and challenges during menopause.

On Facebook, there are dedicated groups where women can join for free, participate in discussions, and organise meet-ups. These groups often serve as a safe space for women to talk about their menopausal symptoms, share tips, and encourage each other to stay active. A great one to look out for is, the "Women Walking for Health" group has thousands of members who regularly post about their walking routines, share motivational quotes, and organise local events. The sense of community and support that these groups offer can be incredibly empowering, helping women to feel less isolated during menopause.

Instagram also plays a significant role in promoting women's health. Many influencers and fitness enthusiasts share their journeys, often targeting women going through menopause. These posts can be inspiring, offering practical advice on how to start and maintain a routine. Hashtags like #Menopause, #WomenWalkingTogether, and #ActiveAfter40 has become popular, allowing women to connect with others on a similar journey. The visual nature of Instagram makes it easy to share progress, celebrate milestones, and find inspiration from others.

The Role of a Balanced Diet in Managing Menopausal Symptoms

While staying active is a big part of managing menopause, what you eat plays an equally important role in how you feel during this time. As a mum that is always on the go, it's easy to grab whatever is quick and convenient, but making a few smart changes to your diet can really help with some of the more frustrating menopausal symptoms—like weight gain, hot flashes, and those unpredictable mood swings.

The hormonal shifts we experience during menopause can slow down our metabolism and change how our body stores fat, making it harder to keep the weight off. It's a challenge many of us face, but the good news is that with some thoughtful food choices, you can stay on top of your health and feel more in control of your body. Focus on a balanced diet—plenty of fruits, veggies, lean proteins, and healthy fats—to help manage weight and keep you feeling your best.

Small changes can make a big difference. For example, adding more fibre can improve digestion, and whole foods rich in calcium and vitamin D support bone health, which becomes more important as we get older. And let's not forget hydration! Drinking enough water can help ease some menopausal symptoms like bloating and fatigue. It's not about going on a strict diet or depriving yourself, but about making simple, informed choices that support your health and energy levels as you navigate this phase of life.

Importance of a Nutrient-Dense Diet

A nutrient-dense diet is one that provides a high concentration of essential vitamins, minerals, and other beneficial compounds relative to the number of calories consumed. This type of diet is particularly important during menopause, as it helps to address the increased nutritional needs that arise from hormonal changes. Key nutrients to focus on include calcium, vitamin D, omega-3 fatty acids, and phytoestrogens, all of which play a role in managing menopausal symptoms and maintaining overall health.

As a mum that is always rushing here and there, I agree it's not easy to always go for the healthier options we tend to opt for what's quicker - recently I have been on a journey to improve my health and find it best to prepare my food, lunch or healthy snacks the evening before so to avoid fast food while working or on the go.

Calcium and Vitamin D

Calcium and vitamin D are critical for bone health, especially as women are at a higher risk of osteoporosis during and after menopause due to declining estrogen levels. Calcium-rich foods such as dairy products, leafy green vegetables, and fortified plant-based milk are essential for maintaining bone density. Vitamin D, which is necessary for calcium absorption, can be obtained from sunlight exposure, as well as from foods like oily fish, fortified cereals, and supplements. Ensuring adequate intake of these nutrients can help prevent bone loss and reduce the risk of fractures.

Omega-3 Fatty Acids

Omega-3 fatty acids, found in fatty fish like salmon and mackerel, as well as in flaxseeds, walnuts, and chia seeds, have anti-inflammatory properties that can benefit women during menopause. These healthy fats can help reduce the frequency and severity of hot flashes, as well as support heart health, which is particularly important given the increased risk of cardiovascular disease after menopause. Additionally, omega-3s have been shown to improve mood and cognitive function, which can be beneficial for managing menopausal symptoms such as anxiety and depression.

Phytoestrogens

Phytoestrogens are plant compounds that mimic the effects of estrogen in the body, helping to balance hormone levels naturally. Foods rich in phytoestrogens include soy products (such as tofu, tempeh, and soy milk), flaxseeds, sesame seeds, and legumes. Incorporating these foods into the diet can help alleviate symptoms like hot flashes and night sweats. Studies have shown that women who consume a diet high in phytoestrogens may experience fewer and less severe menopausal symptoms, making these foods a valuable addition to a menopause-friendly diet.

The Role of a Balanced Diet in Weight Management

Weight gain is a common concern during menopause, driven by a combination of hormonal changes, a slower metabolism, and a decrease in muscle mass. A balanced diet that emphasises whole, unprocessed foods can help manage weight more effectively and reduce the risk of associated health issues such as diabetes and cardiovascular disease.

Whole Grains and Fiber

Incorporating whole grains such as oats, quinoa, brown rice, and whole-wheat products into the diet provides a rich source of fibre, which is essential for maintaining a healthy digestive system and managing weight. Fibre helps regulate blood sugar levels, which can reduce cravings and prevent overeating. It also promotes a feeling of fullness, making it easier to control portion sizes and reduce calorie intake. A diet high in whole grains and fibre has been associated with a lower risk of weight gain and obesity, particularly during menopause.

Fruits and Vegetables

Fruits and vegetables are low in calories but high in essential vitamins, minerals, and antioxidants. These foods should form the foundation of a menopause-friendly diet, as they help maintain energy levels, support immune function, and reduce inflammation. The antioxidants found in colourful fruits and vegetables, such as berries, leafy greens, and bell peppers, can also protect against oxidative stress, which is linked to ageing and chronic diseases. Additionally, the high-water content in fruits and vegetables helps with hydration, which can alleviate symptoms like dry skin and fatigue.

Lean Proteins

Including lean proteins in the diet, such as chicken, turkey, fish, eggs, and plant-based proteins like beans and lentils, is important for maintaining muscle mass and supporting metabolism during menopause. Protein also plays a key role in satiety, helping to control appetite and prevent overeating. Women should aim to include a source of protein with every meal to ensure they are getting enough to support their body's needs during menopause. For those following a plant-based diet, options like tofu, tempeh, quinoa, and legumes can provide ample protein while also contributing to overall nutrient intake.

Reducing Processed Foods and Refined Sugars

Processed foods and refined sugars can exacerbate menopausal symptoms such as weight gain, mood swings, and hot flashes. These foods are often high in empty calories, unhealthy fats, and added sugars, which can lead to spikes in blood sugar levels, increased inflammation, and a higher risk of chronic diseases. Reducing the intake of processed foods and refined sugars can help stabilise blood sugar levels, improve mood, and support overall health during menopause.

Avoiding Unhealthy Fats

During menopause, it's crucial to be mindful of the types of fats consumed, as some can be particularly detrimental to health during this stage. The fats that pose the most danger during menopause are trans fats and certain saturated fats. These unhealthy fats can increase the risk of cardiovascular disease, contribute to weight gain, and exacerbate other menopausal symptoms.

- Trans fats are artificially created fats found in many processed foods, such as fried foods, baked goods, margarine, and snack foods. They are formed through the process of hydrogenation, which turns liquid oils into solid fats to increase shelf life and enhance flavour. However, trans fats are known to raise LDL (bad) cholesterol levels while lowering HDL (good) cholesterol, increasing the risk of heart disease, a significant concern during menopause when cardiovascular risks naturally rise due to hormonal changes. Additionally, trans fats can promote inflammation, which may worsen menopausal symptoms like joint pain and mood swings.
- Saturated fats are primarily found in animal products, such as fatty cuts of meat, butter, cheese, and full-fat dairy products, as well as certain tropical oils like coconut oil and palm oil. While not all saturated fats are harmful, excessive consumption can lead to increased cholesterol levels, further elevating the risk

of heart disease. During menopause, when metabolism tends to slow down, consuming too much saturated fat can also contribute to weight gain, which is already a common challenge during this stage of life.

Healthier Fat Choices

To promote better health during menopause, it's essential to replace unhealthy fats with healthier options. These include:

- **Monounsaturated Fats:** Found in olive oil, avocados, and nuts, monounsaturated fats are heart-healthy and can help reduce bad cholesterol levels. They also provide essential fatty acids that support healthy skin and reduce inflammation.
- **Polyunsaturated Fats:** Omega-3 and omega-6 fatty acids, found in fatty fish (such as salmon and mackerel), flaxseeds, chia seeds, and walnuts, are beneficial for heart health and can help reduce the risk of cardiovascular disease. Omega-3s, in particular, have anti-inflammatory properties that may help alleviate menopausal symptoms like joint pain and mood fluctuations.
- Fats from plant sources, such as those found in seeds, nuts, and plant oils (like flaxseed oil and walnut oil), are rich in antioxidants and other nutrients that support overall health during menopause.

By focusing on these healthier fat sources, women can better manage their weight, reduce the risk of heart disease, and support their overall well-being during menopause. Making mindful dietary choices can lead to improved physical and mental health, making the transition through menopause smoother and more manageable.

Limiting Alcohol and Caffeine

Limiting alcohol and caffeine can play a significant role in managing menopausal symptoms. Both substances are known to exacerbate issues such as hot flashes, sleep disturbances, and anxiety, which are common during menopause. While it might not be necessary to completely eliminate alcohol and caffeine, reducing their intake can make a noticeable difference in symptom management. For women who are sensitive to caffeine, switching to herbal teas or decaffeinated options can be a helpful alternative. Herbal teas like chamomile, peppermint, or ginger offer soothing effects and can be enjoyed without the stimulating impact of caffeine. These teas can also support digestion, reduce stress, and promote better sleep, making them an excellent replacement for caffeinated beverages.

I know for some of us reducing alcohol & caffeine sounds like hard work especially for those of us that enjoy a coffee a few times throughout the day but moderation is key. However, by doing so, some women may find that reducing alcohol intake can significantly reduce the frequency and intensity of hot flashes and improve sleep quality. Opting for lower-sugar options like dry wines or spirits without added mixers can also help manage weight and reduce the risk of exacerbating other menopausal symptoms.

For those looking to eliminate alcohol and caffeine entirely, there are several alternatives that can still provide a satisfying experience. Mocktails, for example, are a great way to enjoy a flavourful beverage without the alcohol. These can be made with fresh fruits, sparkling water, and herbs, providing a refreshing and healthy alternative. Similarly, caffeine-free coffee substitutes, such as roasted chicory root or dandelion tea, can offer a similar taste and comfort without the stimulating effects of caffeine. Incorporating these replacements into daily life can help us manage menopausal symptoms more effectively while still enjoying a variety of flavourful and satisfying beverages. By making mindful choices and exploring new options, it's possible to maintain a balanced and enjoyable lifestyle during this transition.

Hydration and Menopause

Staying hydrated plays a crucial role in managing menopausal symptoms, offering a simple yet effective way to alleviate some of the discomforts associated with this stage of life. Menopause brings about a host of changes in the body, many of which can be exacerbated by dehydration. By ensuring adequate water intake, women can help their bodies navigate these changes more smoothly. One of the key benefits of staying hydrated during menopause is the regulation of body temperature. Hot flashes, a common and often uncomfortable symptom of menopause, can be particularly distressing. When the body is dehydrated, it struggles to regulate temperature effectively, potentially making hot flashes more intense and frequent. Drinking enough water helps the body cool down naturally, reducing the severity of these episodes and providing relief.

In addition to temperature regulation, proper hydration supports digestive health. Menopause can lead to changes in the digestive system, including slower digestion and an increased likelihood of constipation. Water aids in digestion by helping to break down food, absorb nutrients, and move waste through the intestines. Adequate hydration keeps the digestive system functioning optimally, reducing the risk of constipation and promoting overall digestive comfort. Hydration is also vital for maintaining healthy skin, a concern for many women during menopause. As estrogen levels decline, skin can become dry, thin, and less elastic, leading to an increased appearance of fine lines and wrinkles. Drinking plenty of water helps to keep the skin hydrated from the inside out, improving its texture and resilience. Hydrated skin is more supple, less prone to irritation, and better able to withstand the effects of ageing.

Dehydration, on the other hand, can exacerbate several menopausal symptoms. For instance, fatigue is a common issue during menopause, and dehydration can make this fatigue worse. When the body lacks sufficient water, it struggles to perform even basic functions efficiently, leading to feelings of tiredness and lethargy. By staying hydrated, women can boost their energy levels and improve their overall sense of well-being.

Dry skin is another symptom that dehydration can worsen. Without adequate water, the skin's natural moisture barrier is compromised, leading to increased dryness and sensitivity. This can be particularly problematic during menopause when the skin is already more vulnerable due to hormonal changes. Drinking enough water helps to replenish moisture levels in the skin, reducing dryness and enhancing its natural glow. Moreover, dehydration can have a negative impact on mood and cognitive function, both of which are areas of concern during menopause. Research has shown that even mild dehydration can lead to difficulty concentrating, mood swings, and irritability. These symptoms can compound the emotional and psychological challenges many women face during menopause, making it even more important to prioritise hydration.

To ensure adequate hydration, women should aim to drink water regularly throughout the day, rather than waiting until they feel thirsty. Thirst is often a sign that the body is already dehydrated, so it's best to be proactive about water intake. Incorporating a variety of fluids, such as herbal teas and water-rich foods like fruits and vegetables, can also contribute to overall hydration.

Water and Herbal Teas

Water should be the primary source of hydration, but herbal teas can also be beneficial, particularly those that contain soothing ingredients like chamomile, peppermint, or ginger. These teas can help with digestion, reduce stress, and promote relaxation, which can be particularly helpful for managing sleep disturbances. Women should aim to drink at least 8 glasses of water a day, and more if they are physically active or live in a hot climate.

Avoiding Sugary Beverages

Sugary beverages such as sodas, energy drinks, and even fruit juices can have a significant impact on weight management and blood sugar levels, particularly during menopause. These drinks often contain high levels of added sugars, which can lead to weight gain and trigger blood sugar fluctuations. Such fluctuations can, in turn, exacerbate menopausal symptoms like hot flashes, fatigue, and mood swings, making them more difficult to manage. Opting for healthier alternatives can make a substantial difference in managing these symptoms. Water remains the best choice for staying hydrated and maintaining overall health, as it is free of calories and sugars. Drinking plenty of water throughout the day helps regulate body temperature, support digestion, and keep the skin hydrated all of which are crucial for managing menopausal symptoms. Herbal teas are another excellent alternative to sugary drinks. They come in a variety of flavours and can offer additional health benefits, such as calming effects, improved digestion, and enhanced sleep quality. Herbal teas like peppermint, chamomile, and hibiscus are naturally free of caffeine and sugar, making them an ideal choice for women looking to manage their symptoms more effectively. For those who enjoy a bit of flavour in their drinks, infused water is a great option. Adding slices of fruit, such as lemon, lime, or berries, along with fresh herbs like mint or basil, can transform plain water into a refreshing and flavorful beverage without the added sugars. These natural infusions not only provide a burst of flavour but also contribute to hydration and can be a pleasant way to enjoy water throughout the day. By reducing the intake of sugary beverages and replacing them with healthier options like water, herbal teas, or infused water, women can better manage their weight, stabilise blood sugar levels, and alleviate some of the more challenging symptoms of menopause. These small changes in daily habits can lead to a significant improvement in overall well-being during this transitional period.

Managing Stress and Promoting Relaxation

Incorporating phytoestrogens into the diet is another strategy for managing menopausal symptoms. Phytoestrogens are plant compounds that mimic the effects of oestrogen in the body, helping to balance hormone levels naturally. Foods rich in phytoestrogens include soy products, flaxseeds, and legumes. Studies have shown that women who consume a diet high in phytoestrogens may experience fewer hot flashes and other menopausal symptoms. However, it's important to consult with a healthcare provider before making significant changes to the diet, especially if there are any underlying health conditions.

Benefits of a Balanced Diet

The benefits of a balanced diet during menopause extend beyond symptom management. A nutrient-rich diet can also support long-term health by reducing the risk of chronic diseases such as heart disease, diabetes, and osteoporosis. A balanced diet can also improve energy levels and mental clarity, making it easier to stay active and engaged in daily life. Many women find that by making small, sustainable changes to their diet, they can significantly improve their overall well-being during menopause. For instance, replacing sugary snacks with fresh fruit or nuts can help maintain steady blood sugar levels, reducing the likelihood of energy crashes and mood swings.

Moreover, a balanced diet can support weight management, which is often a concern during menopause. By focusing on portion control and choosing nutrient-dense foods, women can maintain a healthy weight without feeling deprived. Simple strategies like eating smaller, more frequent meals throughout the day, and avoiding late-night snacking can also help regulate appetite and prevent overeating. Finally, a balanced diet can enhance the effectiveness of other lifestyle changes, such as regular physical activity. When combined with a consistent exercise routine, a healthy diet can optimise the body's ability to manage stress, maintain muscle mass, and support cardiovascular health. This holistic approach to health and wellness can help us navigate the challenges of menopause with greater ease and confidence.

Integrating Physical Activity and Diet for Optimal Health

To achieve optimal health during menopause, it's essential to integrate both physical activity and a balanced diet into daily life. While each of these components is beneficial on its own, they work synergistically to enhance overall well-being. By adopting a holistic approach to health, women can effectively manage menopausal symptoms and support long-term health.

Holistic Approach

A holistic approach to managing menopause involves creating a daily routine that incorporates both exercise and mindful eating. This routine should be tailored to individual needs and preferences, taking into account factors such as fitness level, dietary restrictions, and personal goals. For example, a woman who enjoys running might schedule daily runs in the morning, followed by a nutritious breakfast rich in protein and fibre. This routine can set a positive tone for the day, providing energy and focus for other activities.

In addition to daily routines, it's important to set realistic goals and track progress. For instance, you might set goals for the number of steps you want to take each day, or for the types of foods they want to include in their diet. Tracking progress through a journal or an app can provide motivation and help identify areas for improvement. Celebrating small victories, such as reaching a weekly exercise goal or trying a new healthy recipe, can also boost confidence and encourage continued efforts.

Practical Tips

To make physical activity and healthy eating a sustainable part of life, it's important to find enjoyable activities and foods. For those of us who enjoy socialising might find that joining social groups is a fun way to stay active while making new friends. Those who enjoy cooking might experiment with new recipes that incorporate healthy ingredients like fresh vegetables, whole grains, and lean proteins. By focusing on activities and foods that bring joy, it's easier to maintain healthy habits over the long term.

Another practical tip is to plan ahead. Preparing meals and snacks in advance can help ensure that healthy options are always available, reducing the temptation to reach for processed or unhealthy foods. Similarly, scheduling time for exercise in the calendar can help make it a priority, even on busy days. For example, setting aside 30 minutes each day for a walk or a yoga session can provide consistency and help establish a routine.

It's also important to listen to the body and make adjustments as needed as some of you may find that you need more rest or lighter exercise on certain days, especially if you are experiencing fatigue or other symptoms. Similarly, dietary needs may change over time, and it's important to be flexible and willing to try new approaches. Consulting with healthcare providers, such as a dietitian or a fitness trainer, can provide personalised guidance and support. In addition to walking groups, other social activities such as group fitness classes, cooking workshops, or health seminars can provide opportunities to connect with others and learn new skills. These activities can also reinforce the importance of a holistic approach to health, as participants can share tips and strategies for maintaining an active lifestyle and a balanced diet. This holistic approach provides a foundation for long-term well-being, helping you to feel empowered and confident as you navigate this important life stage.

Menopause is a significant life transition that requires a proactive approach to health and wellness. By staying active, connecting with supportive communities, and making informed dietary choices, we can effectively manage the symptoms of menopause and support our overall well-being. Physical activity, particularly through participation in women's activity or creative groups, offers both physical and emotional benefits, helping to alleviate symptoms and enhance quality of life. A balanced diet, rich in essential nutrients and free from processed foods, can further support health during menopause, reducing the risk of chronic diseases and promoting long-term wellness. As women navigate this stage of life, it's important to remember that small, consistent changes can make a significant difference. By integrating physical activity and a healthy diet into daily routines, we can take control of their health and well-being, enjoying a vibrant and active life during and after menopause.

References

NHS Inform, Menopause and physical activity

American Heart Association, Good cholesterol and bad cholesterol

Chapter 4: Embracing Self-Care and Personal Growth

As a mother and a mature one at that, I know I am not alone when I say as mothers, we often juggle multiple roles—nurturers, professionals, partners, and caretakers of our households. Amidst this whirlwind of responsibilities, it's easy to forget the most crucial role: taking care of ourselves. Self-care is not an indulgence but a fundamental necessity that allows us to function at our best. In this chapter, we will explore how to prioritise self-care and embrace personal growth, even when life feels chaotic. Self-care is often misunderstood as a luxury—something we indulge in when we have extra time or resources. However, this view is far from the truth. Self-care is not an optional extra; it's a fundamental necessity that enables us to function at our best. When we prioritise our well-being, we are better equipped to handle the demands of our daily lives, to be present for our families, and to excel in our careers.

Without self-care, the constant pressure to fulfil multiple roles can lead to burnout, stress, and a decline in both physical and mental health. Neglecting our own needs doesn't just impact us; it affects everyone around us. When we are drained and exhausted, we can't give our best to our loved ones or our work.

Prioritising Me Time

Self-care encompasses more than just physical health; it involves nurturing our mental, emotional and spiritual well-being. Below are strategies to help you integrate self-care into your busy life. "Me Time" is the practice of setting aside dedicated periods for yourself to unwind, recharge, and engage in activities that you find enjoyable and fulfilling. This practice is crucial for maintaining both mental and physical well-being. By taking breaks from daily responsibilities and stressors, you can significantly reduce burnout and stress. Additionally, carving out time for yourself can enhance mental health by helping to alleviate anxiety and depression.

When you're well-rested and refreshed, you're naturally more productive and focused in other areas of your life. This personal time also contributes to healthier relationships, as it allows you to be more patient and empathetic with others. Beyond that, "Me Time" provides valuable opportunities for self-discovery and growth, helping you gain a better understanding of your needs and desires. It can even spark creativity and innovation, as engaging in hobbies and interests often stimulates new ideas. Integrating "Me Time" into your routine is a proactive way to prioritise your well-being and achieve a more balanced and fulfilling life.

Schedule "Me Time

Just as you schedule work meetings and family activities, it's essential to allocate specific times for yourself. Whether it's reading a book, taking a leisurely walk, shopping -not for food, good old fashion, or simply enjoying a quiet cup of tea, these moments of "me time" are vital for recharging your energy and maintaining your mental health. Consider it a non-negotiable appointment with yourself that you commit to regularly.

Seek Support

Never hesitate to ask for help. Support systems—whether they are family, friends, or professionals— share babysitting with close friends taking turns; these are crucial for managing the pressures of motherhood and work. Sharing household duties with your partner or older children can lighten your load, while seeking professional help, such as a therapist or a coach, can provide valuable insights and coping strategies. Building a network of support ensures that you don't have to carry the weight of your responsibilities alone.

Pursuing Personal Growth

Personal growth is an ongoing journey that doesn't stop at any particular age. It's about continuously evolving, learning, and striving to become the best version of yourself. Here are ways to focus on your growth.

Learning New Skills

Continuing to learn and develop new skills can be both fulfilling and invigorating. Whether you're picking up a new hobby, enrolling in a course, or pursuing a certification related to your career, continuous learning keeps your mind sharp and engaged. It also provides a sense of accomplishment and progress, which can be particularly rewarding during periods of transition or uncertainty.

Setting Goals

Goal-setting is an essential part of personal growth. By defining what you want to achieve in various areas of your life—be it career, family, health, or personal interests—you create a roadmap that gives you direction and purpose. Set realistic, achievable goals that align with your values and aspirations, and break them down into smaller, manageable steps. Regularly reviewing and adjusting your goals as needed ensures that they remain relevant and motivating.

Each year, I set a unique personal challenge—distinct from my usual goals, dreams, or aspirations. This challenge is something entirely outside my routine, an experience I've never tried before. In past years, these challenges have included skydiving, completing the disciplined 75 Hard program over 2.5 months, and, as you know, running a half marathon this year. While I'm not suggesting that others take the same path, setting an annual challenge gives me something to focus on, look forward to, and ultimately brings a strong sense of achievement and vitality. I take time to reflect on each experience and note how it impacted me. After this year's run, I'm already considering doing it again next year with a goal to beat my current time.

Reflection and Journaling

Journaling is a powerful tool for self-reflection and personal development. By writing down your thoughts, emotions, and experiences, you gain deeper insights into your inner world. This practice can help you process complex feelings, identify patterns in your behaviour, and explore new perspectives. Journaling also serves as a record of your growth journey, allowing you to look back and appreciate how far you've come.

Finding Balance

In today's fast-paced world, finding balance between self-care, personal growth, and daily responsibilities can seem like a daunting task. However, achieving this balance is crucial for maintaining overall well-being and living a fulfilling life. The good news is that with some thoughtful strategies and mindful practices, it's possible to strike a harmonious balance that allows you to thrive in all aspects of your life. Below, we'll explore three essential strategies to help you find this balance: delegating and sharing responsibilities, simplifying your life, and celebrating small wins.

Delegating and Sharing Responsibilities

One of the most effective ways to achieve balance in your life is through the delegation of tasks and the sharing of responsibilities. Whether in a family setting, at work, or in social circles, sharing the load can lighten your burden and create a more collaborative and supportive environment. Delegation is not just about offloading tasks; it's about empowering others to contribute and take ownership of their roles. In a family context, for example, involving your children in household chores or meal preparation can teach them valuable life skills such as independence, responsibility, and teamwork. These tasks can be age-appropriate, ensuring that everyone has a role to play that suits their capabilities. This not only reduces your workload but also fosters a sense of shared purpose and cooperation within the family.

In a professional setting, delegating tasks to colleagues or team members allows you to focus on higher-priority responsibilities that require your unique expertise. Effective delegation requires clear communication and trust in others' abilities, which can lead to more efficient workflows and a more harmonious work environment.

While delegation is a powerful tool, it can be challenging for those who are used to handling everything on their own. Common barriers include a fear of losing control, concerns about others' capabilities, or simply the habit of doing things independently. However, learning to delegate effectively is a crucial step toward achieving balance. Start by identifying tasks that others can handle without compromising quality. Provide clear instructions and set expectations, but resist the urge to micromanage. Trust is key—believing in others' abilities and allowing them the space to complete tasks in their way fosters a sense of ownership and accountability. Delegating not only frees up your time but also contributes to the personal growth of those you delegate to, as they learn new skills and take on more responsibility. In the long run, this creates a more balanced and efficient environment for everyone involved.

Simplify Your Life

In our modern lives, it's easy to become overwhelmed by the sheer number of commitments, tasks, and responsibilities we juggle daily. Simplification is a powerful strategy to combat this overwhelm and create more space for what truly matters. Simplifying your life involves evaluating your current commitments and identifying areas where you can reduce complexity. This could mean letting go of activities or obligations that no longer serve you or align with your values. For instance, if you find that certain social commitments are draining your energy without providing any real value, consider scaling back or politely declining future invitations.

Simplification also extends to your physical environment. A cluttered space can contribute to a cluttered mind, making it difficult to focus and relax. Decluttering your home and creating an organised, peaceful environment can significantly reduce stress and increase your sense of well-being. This might involve cleaning out closets, organising your workspace, or adopting minimalist principles in your home decor.

Streamlining Daily Routines

In addition to decluttering your environment, streamlining your daily routines can also help simplify your life. Consider how you start and end your day. Are there habits or routines that could be optimised to save time and reduce stress? For example, preparing meals in advance or laying out your clothes the night before can make your mornings smoother and less rushed.

Digital clutter is another area where simplification can be beneficial. Unsubscribe from unnecessary emails, organise your digital files, and set boundaries around your use of technology. By reducing the number of distractions and interruptions, you create more mental space for focused work and relaxation. Simplifying your life is not about doing less, but about doing more of what matters. It's about creating a life that aligns with your values and priorities, allowing you to invest your time and energy in the things that bring you joy and fulfilment.

Celebrate Small Wins

In the pursuit of balance, it's easy to become fixated on long-term goals and overlook the progress you're making along the way. Celebrating small wins is a powerful practice that helps maintain motivation and fosters a positive outlook. Small wins are the incremental achievements that move you closer to your larger goals. They could be as simple as completing a task on your to-do list, sticking to a new habit for a week, or successfully navigating a challenging situation. While these achievements may seem minor in the grand scheme of things, they play a crucial role in building momentum and reinforcing positive behaviour. When you take the time to acknowledge and celebrate these small victories, you create a sense of progress and accomplishment. This positive reinforcement boosts your motivation and helps you stay committed to your goals, even when the road ahead seems long and challenging.

Practical Ways to Celebrate Small Wins

Celebrating small wins doesn't have to be elaborate or time-consuming. It can be as simple as taking a moment to reflect on your progress, giving yourself a pat on the back, or sharing your achievement with a friend or loved one. Some people find it helpful to keep a journal where they record their daily wins, no matter how small. This practice not only reinforces positive behaviour but also provides a tangible record of your progress over time. Another effective way to celebrate small wins is to reward yourself with something that brings you joy. This could be a small treat, a relaxing activity, or simply taking a break to enjoy something you love. The key is to make the celebration meaningful and aligned with your values.

By regularly celebrating small wins, you cultivate a mindset of positivity and resilience. This not only helps you stay motivated but also enhances your overall sense of well-being, making it easier to maintain balance in your life. This may seem obvious to many, yet I'm certain most of us rarely, if ever, practise it. We seldom pause to acknowledge moments where we handle things well or pull everything together against the odds. As mothers, we often view our efforts simply as responsibilities, overlooking how truly remarkable we are—yes, remarkable—and rarely thinking to reward ourselves for it.

Finding Your Unique Balance

While the strategies of delegating responsibilities, simplifying your life, and celebrating small wins are universally applicable, it's important to recognize that finding balance is a highly personal journey. What works for one person may not work for another, and your needs may change over time as your circumstances evolve.

Self-Reflection and Mindfulness

A key component of finding balance is self-reflection. Regularly check in with yourself to assess how you're feeling and whether your current routines and responsibilities are aligned with your values and priorities. Mindfulness practices, such as meditation or journaling, can help you develop greater self-awareness and make more intentional choices about how you spend your time and energy. If you find that you're constantly feeling overwhelmed or out of balance, it may be time to reassess your commitments and make adjustments. This could involve setting new boundaries, saying no to additional responsibilities, or seeking support from others.

Flexibility and Adaptability

Another important aspect of finding balance is flexibility. Life is unpredictable, and circumstances can change quickly. Being adaptable and willing to adjust your approach as needed is key to maintaining balance over the long term. For example, during particularly busy periods at work, you may need to temporarily scale back on personal projects or social commitments to prevent burnout. Conversely, during quieter times, you may have more capacity to invest in personal growth or self-care activities. The ability to adjust your priorities and expectations in response to changing circumstances is a crucial skill for achieving and maintaining balance.

Setting Realistic Expectations

It's also important to set realistic expectations for yourself. Balance doesn't mean that every aspect of your life will be perfectly aligned at all times. There will be periods when certain areas require more attention than others, and that's okay. The goal is not to achieve a perfect equilibrium but to create a sense of harmony that allows you to navigate life's challenges with grace and resilience. Being kind to yourself and recognizing that balance is an ongoing process can help reduce feelings of guilt or inadequacy when things don't go as planned. Remember that it's okay to seek help or take a step back when needed—self-compassion is an essential component of maintaining balance.

Chapter 5: Health and Fitness

In today's fast-paced world, where so much of our time is spent sitting—whether it's working, driving, or just scrolling through our phones—it's more important than ever to keep moving. And as busy mums, finding time for regular physical activity isn't always easy, but it's so worth it. Exercise isn't just about losing weight or toning up—it's about boosting your overall well-being, both physically and mentally.

When we talk about staying active, it doesn't have to mean intense gym sessions or strict workout routines. Regular movement can look different for everyone, and it's all about finding what works for you. It could be a quick walk around the block before picking up the children, a fitness class to stretch out those tired muscles, or even something as simple as playing with your children at the park. Whether it's cardio to get your heart pumping, strength training to build muscle, or even gardening to break a sweat, each small effort adds up.

The key is to make it a habit, something you enjoy, and something that fits into your busy schedule. By staying active, you're not only caring for your body, but also giving yourself the mental and emotional boost you need to tackle everything else that's on your plate. So don't think of it as one more thing to check off your list—think of it as a way to recharge and feel good in your own skin.

Why Regular Exercise Matters

The human body is made for movement. If we think back to earlier times, our ancestors were naturally active, whether they were hunting, gathering, or working the land. Physical exertion was simply part of daily life. Today, however, the world looks very different. With modern conveniences making tasks easier, many of us lead more sedentary lifestyles, and while technology has brought incredible improvements, it has also led to a rise in health issues like obesity, type 2 diabetes, and heart disease. For us mums, it can be easy to get swept up in the whirlwind of family and work, but finding ways to stay active is crucial. Regular exercise isn't just about physical health; it's a powerful tool for your overall well-being.

Staying active can help counteract the effects of modern life, offering benefits that go far beyond the surface. Exercise boosts your energy levels, improves your mood, and helps you manage stress more effectively—essential when you're juggling. It strengthens your heart, supports healthy weight management, and reduces the risk of long-term health issues. But it's also about giving yourself the mental and emotional recharge you need to feel your best. Finding time for movement, whether through a structured workout or something as simple as a walk, allows you to take control of your health and well-being in a way that will benefit both you and your family.

1. **Cardiovascular Health:** One of the most significant benefits of regular exercise is its positive impact on cardiovascular health. The heart, like any other muscle, needs to be exercised to stay strong and efficient. Aerobic activities, such as walking, running, cycling, or swimming, increase the heart rate, which in turn strengthens the heart muscle and improves blood circulation. This reduces the risk of heart disease, lowers blood pressure, and helps manage cholesterol levels.
   A study published in the *Journal of the American College of Cardiology* found that even moderate-intensity exercise, such as brisk walking for 30 minutes a day, can significantly reduce the risk of coronary heart disease. The researchers concluded that regular physical activity plays a crucial role in both the prevention and management of cardiovascular conditions.

2. **Mental Health and Cognitive Function:** Exercise is not just beneficial for your body; it also has profound effects on your mind. Physical activity stimulates the release of endorphins, referred to as "feel-good" hormones, which can help alleviate symptoms of depression, anxiety, and stress. Regular exercise has been shown to improve mood, boost self-esteem, and enhance overall mental well-being.
   In addition to its mood-boosting effects, exercise also enhances cognitive function. According to research published in *The Lancet Psychiatry*, regular physical activity is associated with improved memory, faster learning, and a reduced risk of cognitive decline. Exercise increases blood flow to the brain, promoting the growth of new neurons and supporting brain plasticity, which is crucial for learning and memory.

3. **Weight Management:** Weight management is often the primary motivator for many of us when it comes to regular exercise, and with good reason. Staying active helps burn calories, which is essential for both shedding excess weight and maintaining a healthy one. But the benefits of exercise in managing weight go far beyond just burning calories.

   For instance, strength training is incredibly valuable as it builds lean muscle mass, which naturally boosts your metabolism. This means that even when you're not working out, your body is burning more calories at rest. Exercise also plays an important role in regulating hormones like insulin and leptin, both of which help manage your appetite and how your body stores fat.

   That said, while exercise is a key part of weight management, it works best when paired with a balanced, nourishing diet. Relying solely on exercise without addressing what you eat may not lead to the results you're looking for. It's about creating a healthy combination of movement and mindful eating that can help you reach and maintain your goals, all while boosting your overall health and well-being.

4. **Bone and Muscle Health:** As we get older and juggle the demands of motherhood, it's easy to overlook the changes happening in our bodies, like the natural weakening of bones and muscles. Staying active is not only about keeping up with our children but also about protecting our health in the long run. Regular exercise, particularly weight-bearing and resistance exercises, is key to maintaining bone density and muscle mass. Simple activities like dancing with your little ones, or even light jogging can help keep your bones strong. Resistance training, like lifting weights or using resistance bands, strengthens muscles, improves balance, and reduces the risk of falls—something that becomes more important as we age.

   A study published in the Journal of Bone and Mineral Research found that adults who regularly engage in resistance training have a lower risk of developing osteoporosis. As mothers, this means fitting strength exercises into your routine can go a long way in keeping your body strong and capable—especially as we handle life's busy and active demands.

5. **Improved Sleep Quality:** Regular exercise can lead to better sleep, which is essential for maintaining overall health—especially when balancing the demands of motherhood. Physical activity helps regulate your body's natural sleep-wake cycle, making it easier to fall asleep and stay asleep through the night. It also increases the time spent in deep sleep, the phase that is most restorative for your body and mind.

   A study published in Sleep Medicine Reviews found that moderate-to-vigorous physical activity significantly improves sleep quality and reduces the time it takes to fall asleep. The study also highlighted that regular exercise can help ease symptoms of insomnia and other sleep-related issues, offering a natural way to improve sleep for busy mums who need all the rest they can get.

6. **Enhanced Immune Function:** Regular exercise has been shown to boost the immune system, making you less susceptible to infections and illnesses. Physical activity promotes the circulation of immune cells, which helps the body detect and fight off pathogens more effectively.

   Research from the *American Journal of Medicine* indicates that individuals who engage in regular, moderate exercise have a lower incidence of upper respiratory tract infections compared to sedentary individuals. However, it's important to note that extreme exercise, such as training for a marathon, can temporarily suppress immune function, so moderation is key.

Home Exercise Options

One of the biggest challenges for us mums, when we are already exhausted, is finding time to squeeze in exercise between juggling work, family, and personal commitments. Luckily, there are plenty of effective workouts you can do at home, often requiring little to no equipment. YouTube is a fantastic resource for free exercise videos that cater to different fitness levels and preferences.

For a quick and effective workout, High-Intensity Interval Training (HIIT) is ideal. These workouts involve short, intense bursts of activity followed by brief rest periods, allowing you to burn calories and boost cardiovascular health in 10 to 30 minutes. Channels like FitnessBlender and PopSugar Fitness offer a variety of HIIT routines that fit into even the busiest schedules.

One of the best aspects of these workouts is that they're not only free and accessible directly on your TV, but they also offer a wide variety to suit all fitness levels—and even allow the whole family to join in. I think back to the COVID-19 pandemic lockdown with my son, then four years old, and I would follow Joe Wicks' daily exercise routines on YouTube, just like so many others worldwide. My son loved participating and eagerly looked forward to our mornings spent exercising with Joe.

If you're looking to unwind while improving flexibility and strength, Yoga or Pilates are excellent options. Channels like Yoga with Adriene and Pilates Body Raven feature sessions ranging from 10 minutes to over an hour, making it easy to find a moment to practise, whether it's in the morning or after the children are in bed.

Strength training is also important for maintaining muscle mass and boosting metabolism. Channels like HASfit and Sydney Cummings provide routines that can be done with or without weights, allowing you to adapt based on your space and equipment. For those who love to dance, fun routines from The Fitness Marshall and POPSUGAR Fitness make exercise enjoyable and a great way to relieve stress after a long day.

Creating a Home Gym

You don't need an extensive home gym to get a great workout. A few basic pieces of equipment can enhance your home workouts significantly:

- Resistance bands: These are versatile, inexpensive, and excellent for strength training.
- Dumbbells: A set of adjustable dumbbells can be used for a variety of exercises.
- Yoga mat: Essential for floor exercises, stretching, yoga and Pilates.
- Stability ball: Great for core exercises and adding variety to your workouts.
- Skipping rope: An effective tool for cardio workouts.

Hydration

Staying hydrated is crucial for maintaining optimal health. Dehydration can lead to a range of issues, including headaches, fatigue, dizziness, and poor concentration. Therefore, it's essential to drink enough water throughout the day to stay hydrated Water plays a vital role in many bodily functions, including:

- Regulating body temperature: Through sweating and respiration.
- Supporting digestion: Aiding in the breakdown and absorption of nutrients.
- Maintaining kidney function: Helping to remove waste products from the body.
- Lubricating joints: Keeping them flexible and functioning properly.
- Transporting nutrients: Ensuring that vitamins and minerals reach the cells where they are needed.

Tips for Staying Hydrated

Here are some practical tips to help you stay hydrated:

- **Start your day with lemon water:** Drinking a glass of warm water with lemon first thing in the morning can kickstart your metabolism and hydrate your body after a night's sleep. Lemon water is also a great source of vitamin C and can aid digestion.
- **Carry a water bottle:** Having a reusable water bottle with you throughout the day makes it easier to sip water regularly.
- **Set reminders:** Use your phone or a hydration app to remind you to drink water at regular intervals.

- **Infuse your water:** If you find plain water boring, try infusing it with fruits, vegetables, or herbs like cucumber, mint, berries, or citrus fruits to add flavour without adding sugar or calories.
- **Eat water-rich foods:** Foods like cucumbers, watermelons, oranges, and strawberries have high water content and can contribute to your daily hydration needs.

The Benefits of Lemon Water

Lemon water is a simple yet powerful way to enhance your hydration routine. Here are some benefits of incorporating lemon water into your daily regimen:

- Lemons are high in vitamin C, which is known to support the immune system.
- Lemon water can help improve digestion and relieve symptoms of indigestion and bloating.
- The citric acid in lemons helps to flush out toxins and supports liver function.
- The antioxidants in lemon water can help reduce skin blemishes and wrinkles, promoting a healthy, glowing complexion.
- The scent of lemon has mood-enhancing properties, and drinking lemon water can help boost energy levels naturally.

Nutritious Habits: Eating for Health

The Power of Smoothies

Smoothies are an excellent way to pack a lot of nutrition into a quick and convenient meal or snack. They are particularly beneficial for active mums who need a fast, nutritious option that can be prepared in minutes. A well-balanced smoothie can provide essential vitamins, minerals, fibre, and protein to keep you energised throughout the day.

Here's a simple guide to creating your healthy smoothie:

1) **Choose a Base:** Start with a liquid base such as water, almond milk, coconut water, or yoghurt. The base should make up about one-third of your smoothie.
2) **Add Fruits and Vegetables:** Incorporate a mix of fruits and vegetables. Aim for a balance of both to ensure you get a variety of nutrients. Some great options include:
   a) Fruits: Bananas, berries, mangoes, pineapples, apples, and pears.
   b) Vegetables: Spinach, kale, cucumbers, carrots, and beets.
3) **Include Protein:** Add a source of protein to make your smoothie more satisfying and nutritious. Options include:
   a) Protein powder: Whey, plant-based, or collagen protein.
   b) Greek yoghurt: Adds creaminess and protein.
   c) Nuts and seeds: Almonds, chia seeds, flaxseeds, or hemp seeds.
4) **Healthy Fats:** Incorporate healthy fats to keep you full longer and support overall health. Good choices are:
   a) Nut butter: Almond, peanut, or cashew butter.
   b) Avocado: Adds a creamy texture and healthy fats.
   c) Coconut oil: A small amount can enhance flavour and provide medium-chain triglycerides (MCTs).
5) **Boosters:** Add superfoods or boosters for extra nutrition. Some popular options include:
   a) Spirulina or chlorella: Rich in vitamins and minerals.
   b) Cacao powder: Provides antioxidants and a chocolate flavour.
   c) Matcha powder: Adds a caffeine boost and antioxidants.
   d) Turmeric: Known for its anti-inflammatory properties.

Green Power Smoothie

Ingredients:

- 1 cup unsweetened almond milk
- 1 banana
- 1/2 cup frozen pineapple chunks
- 1 cup fresh spinach leaves
- 1/4 avocado
- 1 tablespoon chia seeds
- 1 scoop plant-based protein powder
- 1 teaspoon spirulina powder
- Ice cubes (optional)

Instructions:

- Combine all ingredients in a blender.
- Blend until smooth and creamy.
- Adjust the consistency by adding more almond milk or ice cubes, if needed.
- Pour into a glass and enjoy immediately.

Sea Moss Smoothie Recipe

Here's a delicious and nutritious sea moss smoothie recipe that you can easily incorporate into your daily routine:

Ingredients:

- 1 tablespoon sea moss gel
- 1 cup coconut water
- 1/2 cup frozen mango chunks
- 1/2 cup frozen pineapple chunks
- 1/2 banana
- 1 tablespoon chia seeds
- 1/2 teaspoon turmeric powder (optional)
- Ice cubes (optional)

Instructions:

- Combine all ingredients in a blender.
- Blend until smooth and creamy.
- Adjust the consistency by adding more coconut water or ice cubes, if needed.
- Pour into a glass and enjoy immediately.

The Benefits of Sea Moss

Sea moss, also known as Irish moss, is a type of red algae that has been used for centuries for its health benefits. It is packed with essential nutrients and has gained popularity as a superfood. Here are some of the key benefits of sea moss:

1. **Rich in Nutrients**: Sea moss contains 92 of the 102 minerals that the human body needs, including iodine, calcium, potassium, and magnesium.
2. **Supports Immune Health:** The high content of vitamins and antioxidants in sea moss can help strengthen the immune system.
3. **Promotes Digestive Health:** Sea moss is a natural source of dietary fibre, which supports healthy digestion and regular bowel movements.

4. **Enhances Skin Health:** The vitamins and minerals in sea moss can help improve skin health, reducing inflammation and promoting a clear complexion.
5. **Boosts Energy Levels:** The nutrients in sea moss can help increase energy levels and combat fatigue.
6. **Supports Thyroid Function:** Sea moss is rich in iodine, which is essential for healthy thyroid function and hormone regulation.

Setting Realistic Goals

Consistency is key to achieving and maintaining your health and fitness goals, especially as a mum on the go. Here are some tips to help you stay on track. Start with small, achievable goals that can be gradually increased as you build momentum. This approach prevents burnout and keeps you motivated. Establish a daily or weekly routine that includes dedicated time for exercise, meal prep, and self-care. Making these activities a regular part of your life will help them become habits.

Consider using your journal or an app to track your workouts, water intake, and meals. Monitoring your progress provides motivation and highlights areas for improvement. Sharing your goals with a friend or family member can offer valuable support and encouragement. You might also think about joining a fitness group or an online community for added accountability. Don't forget to acknowledge and celebrate your progress, no matter how small. Recognising your achievements reinforces positive behaviour and helps keep your motivation high.

Overcoming Common Challenges

Maintaining a healthy lifestyle can be challenging, especially for busy mums. Here are some common obstacles and strategies to overcome them:

1. Lack of time: Incorporate short, effective workouts into your routine, such as 10-minute HIIT sessions or quick yoga flows. Make the most of small pockets of time throughout the day.
2. Fatigue: Prioritise rest and recovery by getting adequate sleep and listening to your body. If you're feeling too tired to exercise, opt for gentler activities like stretching or a walk.
3. Motivation: Keep your goals visible by writing them down and placing them in prominent locations. Surround yourself with positive influences, such as motivational quotes or success stories.
4. Limited resources: Utilise free resources like YouTube workout videos and online recipes. You don't need expensive equipment or gym memberships to stay healthy.

Key Takeaways

Health and fitness are essential for feeling balanced and fulfilled, especially for us mums in demand juggling countless responsibilities. Regular exercise isn't just a "nice-to-have" — it's a powerful way to enhance your overall productivity, providing you with the energy and strength to tackle whatever life throws your way. The benefits are abundant: from improving heart health and managing weight to strengthening bones and muscles, boosting your immune system, and even lifting your mood while sharpening your mind.

Exercise isn't solely about transforming your body — it's about revitalising your spirit too. Whether it's taking a brisk walk to collect the children from school, fitting in a quick home workout between errands, or cranking up the music for a lively dance session in the living room, every bit of movement brings you closer to feeling stronger, healthier, and more vibrant.

By making physical activity a regular part of your routine, you're investing in a future where you feel more confident, resilient, and ready to face life's challenges. It's not about perfection or sticking to a strict plan; it's about finding ways to move that suit you, fit into your busy life, and make you feel good. The journey to staying fit is personal, but the rewards are universal: better health, increased energy, and a renewed sense of purpose that will help you thrive in every aspect of your life.

References

The Lancet Psychiatry, Exercise and Improved Brain Memory

American Society of Bone and Mineral Research, Journal of Bone and Mineral Research

American Journal of Medicine, Regular Exercise

Chapter 6: Physical Health Meets Mental Wellness

Regular exercise is often praised for its physical perks, but its mental health benefits are just as significant, especially for busy mums in their 40s navigating life's changes. As we transition into new phases, like menopause, it can feel overwhelming with the emotional and physical symptoms that accompany it—hello, brain fog, hair loss, and those surprise hot flashes! But don't worry; moving your body can be a game changer.

The National Health Service (NHS) suggests that adults aim for at least 150 minutes of moderate-intensity exercise each week. Think of it as carving out time to recharge while boosting your mood. Moderate-intensity activities like brisk walking, cycling on flat paths, or even dancing in the living room are great for getting your heart rate up while still allowing you to chat with a friend. This type of movement helps with cardiovascular health, weight management, and reducing the risk of chronic conditions like heart disease and diabetes.

For those who crave a little extra challenge, vigorous-intensity exercise is where it's at. Running, swimming laps, or tackling those hilly bike rides fit the bill. You'll get a solid workout in less time, making it easier to fit into your schedule. By embracing these NHS recommendations, you're not only nurturing your physical health but also enhancing your mental well-being and overall quality of life—because happy, healthy mums make the best superheroes!

Brain Fog: The Mental Cloud of Menopause

Brain fog refers to a state of mental confusion, forgetfulness, and lack of focus or clarity. During menopause, this symptom can be particularly frustrating as it affects daily functioning and cognitive performance.

- **Causes**: The primary culprit behind brain fog during menopause is the fluctuation of hormones, particularly oestrogen. Oestrogen plays a crucial role in cognitive functions, and as its levels decline, so can a woman's ability to concentrate, remember details, and think clearly.
- **Symptoms**: Women experiencing brain fog may find it challenging to recall recent events, struggle to focus on tasks, or feel mentally fatigued even after adequate rest. This can lead to frustration, anxiety, and even self-doubt as women may feel they are "losing their edge."
- **Management**: Maintaining a healthy lifestyle can help manage brain fog. Regular physical activity, a balanced diet rich in omega-3 fatty acids and antioxidants, adequate sleep, and mental exercises such as puzzles or reading can support cognitive health. I know that some women also find relief through hormone replacement therapy (HRT), but this should be discussed with a healthcare provider.

Hair Loss: The Hidden Impact of Hormonal Imbalance

Hair loss is another common issue women face during menopause. This can manifest as thinning hair, increased shedding, or even bald patches.

- **Causes**: The decrease in oestrogen and progesterone during menopause leads to a slower hair growth cycle and increased hair shedding. Additionally, the body may produce more androgens (male hormones), which can shrink hair follicles and result in hair loss.
- **Symptoms**: Women may notice more hair on their brushes, thinning of hair around the crown or temples, and a general decrease in hair volume. This can be distressing as hair is often closely linked to a woman's sense of identity and femininity.
- **Management**: To manage hair loss, it's important to maintain a diet rich in vitamins and minerals like biotin, vitamin D, and zinc. Gentle hair care routines, avoiding harsh chemicals and heat styling, can also protect hair from further damage. In some cases, treatments like minoxidil or laser therapy might be recommended by a dermatologist.

Hot Flashes: The Fiery Symptom of Menopause

Hot flashes are one of the hallmark symptoms of menopause, affecting up to 75% of women during this stage. These sudden feelings of intense heat can be uncomfortable and often disrupt daily life.

- **Causes**: Hot flashes are believed to be triggered by changes in the hypothalamus, the part of the brain that regulates body temperature. The decline in oestrogen levels during menopause can confuse the hypothalamus, causing it to overreact to slight changes in body temperature and triggering a hot flash.
- **Symptoms**: A hot flash typically begins with a sudden sensation of heat in the upper body, particularly the face, neck, and chest. This may be accompanied by redness of the skin, sweating, and a rapid heartbeat. Hot flashes can last from a few seconds to several minutes and may be followed by chills as the body tries to cool down.
- **Management**: Lifestyle changes such as dressing in layers, staying in cool environments, and avoiding triggers like spicy foods, alcohol, and caffeine can help manage hot flashes. For some women, HRT can significantly reduce the frequency and severity of hot flashes. Non-hormonal medications, such as blood pressure medications, may also provide relief - always consult with your medical practitioner.

The Science Behind Exercise and Mental Health

At the core of exercise's mental health benefits are the physiological changes that occur in the brain during and after physical activity. Endorphins are neurotransmitters that interact with receptors in the brain to reduce the perception of pain and trigger positive feelings. This endorphin release is one reason why many people experience a "runner's high" after intense exercise, a sensation of euphoria and well-being. In addition to endorphins, exercise stimulates the release of other important neurotransmitters, including serotonin and dopamine. Serotonin is associated with mood regulation, and higher levels of serotonin are linked to reduced symptoms of depression and anxiety. Dopamine, often called the "reward" neurotransmitter, plays a key role in motivation and pleasure, reinforcing the desire to engage in activities that are enjoyable or rewarding.

Exercise also promotes the growth of new neurons in the brain, particularly in the hippocampus, an area critical for memory and learning. This process, known as neurogenesis, can enhance cognitive function and protect against age-related cognitive decline. Regular physical activity has been shown to improve memory, increase attention span, and boost problem-solving abilities. As a mature mum I have experienced moments where I leave one room to go and find something and just like that, I have forgotten what I was looking for - it can be so frustrating.

Exercise as a Natural Antidepressant

One of the most compelling reasons to incorporate exercise into daily life is its effectiveness as a natural antidepressant. Depression is a common mental health disorder characterised by persistent feelings of sadness, hopelessness, and a lack of interest in activities once enjoyed. While medication and therapy are often prescribed to manage depression, exercise offers a complementary or alternative treatment with significant benefits.

Research has shown that regular exercise can be as effective as antidepressant medications in reducing symptoms of mild to moderate depression. The mechanisms behind this effect include increased neurotransmitter levels, reduced inflammation, and improved sleep patterns. Exercise also provides a sense of routine and structure, which can be particularly beneficial for individuals struggling with depression. Moreover, the sense of accomplishment that comes from completing a workout, no matter how small, can boost self-esteem and provide a positive counterbalance to the negative thought patterns often associated with depression. The social aspect of exercise, whether through group classes, team sports, or simply going to a gym, can also alleviate feelings of isolation and loneliness, which are common in those with depression.

Reducing Anxiety Through Physical Activity

Anxiety is another widespread mental health issue that can be effectively managed through exercise. Anxiety disorders are characterised by excessive worry, nervousness, and fear, often leading to physical symptoms such as an increased heart rate, sweating, and trembling. While anxiety is a normal response to stress, chronic anxiety can significantly impair a person's quality of life. Exercise has been shown to reduce anxiety symptoms both in the short term and over time. During physical activity, the body undergoes physiological changes that mimic the stress response—elevated heart rate, increased breathing, and the release of stress hormones like cortisol. However, the controlled and predictable nature of exercise helps the body adapt to these changes, leading to improved stress resilience.

In the long term, regular exercise can lead to a reduction in baseline anxiety levels. This is partly due to the enhanced regulation of the body's stress response system. Additionally, exercise-induced improvements in sleep quality can have a significant impact on anxiety, as poor sleep is often both a cause and a consequence of anxiety disorders.

Exercise also serves as a powerful distraction from anxious thoughts. Engaging in physical activity requires focus and concentration, whether it's maintaining proper form during a workout, following the rhythm of a dance class, or partaking in a bike ride. This shift in attention away from worries and toward the present moment can provide immediate relief from anxiety.

Cognitive Benefits and Brain Health

Beyond mood regulation, exercise plays a critical role in maintaining and enhancing cognitive function. Cognitive decline is a natural part of ageing, but regular physical activity can slow this process and even improve certain aspects of cognition. As mentioned earlier, exercise promotes neurogenesis in the hippocampus, which is essential for memory formation and retention. This is particularly important for older adults, as the risk of cognitive decline and neurodegenerative diseases like Alzheimer's increases with age. Studies have shown that physically active individuals have a lower risk of developing dementia and experience slower cognitive decline compared to those who are sedentary.

Exercise also improves executive function, which includes skills such as planning, decision-making, and problem-solving. These cognitive processes are vital for daily life and are often impaired in individuals with mental health disorders. People with depression may struggle with decision-making, while those with ADHD (attention deficit hyperactivity disorder) may find it difficult to plan and organise tasks. Regular physical activity can enhance these cognitive abilities, leading to better overall mental functioning.

Stress reduction and relaxation

Stress is a constant companion in the lives of busy mums, but when it becomes chronic, it can severely impact both mental and physical health, making it difficult to function as a parent. When you're feeling stressed or moody, it not only affects your well-being but also how you interact with your children. Prioritising stress reduction is crucial for being the best parent you can be.

Over time, regular exercise helps train your body to cope better with everyday pressures, resulting in a more balanced and less reactive response to stress. You'll find that you can navigate the challenges of parenting with greater ease.

By incorporating stress-reducing practices into your routine, you not only improve your health but also create a more nurturing environment for your family. Taking care of yourself means you can show up as the patient, joyful, and engaged parent your children need.

Exercise as a Tool For Building Resilience

Mental resilience is the ability to bounce back from adversity and maintain mental well-being in the face of challenges is crucial for coping with life's ups and downs. Exercise is a powerful tool for building resilience, as it strengthens both the body and mind. Engaging in regular physical activity requires discipline, commitment, and the ability to push through discomfort qualities that are transferable to other areas of life. Whether it's completing a challenging workout, attending your local gym, or simply staying consistent with a fitness routine, exercise teaches perseverance and the value of hard work. Moreover, the confidence gained from setting and achieving fitness goals can boost overall self-esteem and provide a sense of control in one's life. This sense of empowerment can be particularly valuable for individuals dealing with mental health challenges, as it reinforces the belief that they have the ability to overcome obstacles and achieve positive outcomes.

Multitasking and Combining Activities

For those with particularly tight schedules, combining exercise with other activities can be a time-efficient way to stay active. For example, if you have young children, you can turn playtime into a workout by engaging in active games, such as playing tag, going for a walk, or having a dance party at home. If you commute to work, consider biking or walking part of the way instead of driving. These small changes can add up, helping you stay active without requiring extra time out of your day. Here's how you can overcome obstacles involved in consistent exercise:

1. Make It Enjoyable

The key thing is to find an exercise routine that you enjoy. Whether it's dancing, swimming, jog, or yoga, choosing an activity you love increases the likelihood that you'll stick with it. Experiment with different forms of exercise until you find something that feels less like a chore and more like a fun part of your day.

2. Schedule Exercise Like an Appointment

Treat exercise as a non-negotiable part of your day by scheduling it just like any other important appointment. Whether it's a morning walk, lunchtime yoga, or an evening gym session, block out time in your calendar and stick to it. Consistency is key to making exercise a habit.

3. Start Small and Build Up

If time or energy is a concern, start with small steps. Even 5-10 minutes of exercise can make a difference. Over time, as you start to feel the benefits, you may find it easier to extend your workouts. The important thing is to start, no matter how small.

4. Find a Workout Buddy

Exercising with a friend, joining a group or gym can provide motivation and accountability. A workout partner can make exercise more enjoyable and encourage you to stay committed, even on days when you feel like skipping it. Plus, it adds a social aspect to your routine, making it more fun.

5. Incorporate Exercise into Daily Activities

If finding time for a dedicated workout is challenging, look for ways to incorporate physical activity into your daily routine. Take the stairs instead of the elevator, walk or bike instead of driving short distances, or do some stretches while watching TV. These small changes can add up and help you stay active.

6. Address Physical Limitations

If physical limitations or chronic health conditions are barriers, consult with a healthcare provider or physical therapist to develop a safe and effective exercise plan. They can help tailor a program that suits your needs and capabilities, ensuring that you can exercise without risking injury.

7. Focus on the Benefits

Remind yourself of the physical and mental health benefits of regular exercise. Whether it's improving your energy levels, boosting your mood, or reducing stress, keeping these positive outcomes in mind can help motivate you to stay active, even when it's challenging.

8. Be Flexible and Adapt

Life is unpredictable, and sometimes your best-laid plans might not work out. Be flexible and willing to adapt your exercise routine as needed. If you miss a workout, don't be discouraged. Instead, look for another opportunity to fit it in, or simply get back on track the next day. Consistency over time is more important than perfection.

9. Reward Yourself

Set up a reward system to celebrate your achievements, no matter how small. Whether it's treating yourself to a new workout outfit, enjoying a relaxing bath, or indulging in a Favourite healthy snack, rewarding yourself can reinforce positive behaviour and keep you motivated.

10. Seek Support

If you're struggling to stay motivated, seek support from others. This could be a personal trainer, a supportive friend, or an online community. Sharing your challenges and successes with others can provide encouragement and help you stay committed to your goals.

11. Reframe Your Mindset

Sometimes, overcoming obstacles is about changing the way you think about exercise. Instead of seeing it as a burden, try to view it as a form of self-care and an investment in your long-term health. A positive mindset can make a significant difference in your motivation and consistency. By identifying and addressing the obstacles to exercising, you can create a sustainable routine that fits your lifestyle. Remember that everyone's journey is unique, and it's okay to face challenges along the way. The key is to stay committed, be patient with yourself, and keep finding ways to make exercise a regular and enjoyable part of your life.

12. Make it a Habit

To build a lasting exercise habit, consider practical strategies backed by research. Wendy Wood's Good Habits, Bad Habits delves into the science of forming positive habits, emphasising how small, consistent actions can lead to meaningful change. The Harvard Business Review (hbr.org) highlights the importance of starting with manageable steps and rewarding progress to reinforce your commitment. By focusing on these incremental improvements, new routines can become second nature, making the habit sustainable over time.

Choosing the Right Type of Exercise

Choosing the right type of exercise as you age is crucial to avoid muscle spasms, injuries, and other issues, especially for women in their 40s. As the body undergoes various changes, such as decreased muscle mass and bone density, it's important to tailor exercise routines to these changes to maintain health and prevent injuries. Consulting a healthcare provider or a physical therapist before starting or modifying an exercise routine is essential. They can assess your overall health, provide recommendations, and ensure that your exercise plan is safe and effective for your specific needs.

As women enter their 40s, bone density may begin to decline, increasing the risk of osteoporosis. Weight-bearing and resistance exercises are beneficial for maintaining bone health, but high-impact activities should be approached with caution to avoid joint stress. Opting for low-impact exercises, such as walking, cycling, or swimming, can reduce stress on the joints while providing cardiovascular benefits. Additionally, incorporating resistance exercises with moderate weights and higher repetitions can help build muscle without overloading the joints. Bodyweight squats, resistance band workouts, and light dumbbell exercises are effective and safer choices.

Maintaining flexibility and mobility is also important to prevent injuries and muscle spasms. Incorporating stretching and mobility exercises into your routine can help. Dynamic stretches, such as leg swings and arm circles, are useful before workouts to warm up the muscles and improve range of motion. After exercise, performing static stretches to lengthen the muscles and enhance flexibility is beneficial. Focus on areas prone to tightness, such as the hamstrings, quads, and lower back.

Enhancing balance and core strength can further help prevent falls and support overall stability. Including balance exercises, such as standing on one leg or using a balance board, can improve stability. Strengthening the core with exercises like planks, bridges, and bird-dogs supports the spine and enhances overall balance.

Starting with lower intensity and gradually increasing the difficulty of your workouts allows your body to adapt and reduces the risk of injury. Progressive overload, or the gradual increase in weight, duration, or intensity of exercises, is important. Avoid making significant changes to your routine too quickly and pay attention to how your body responds to different exercises. If discomfort or pain occurs, it may be necessary to adjust your routine accordingly.

Incorporating adequate recovery time is crucial to prevent overuse injuries and muscle spasms. Include rest days in your exercise routine to allow muscles to recover and repair. On rest days, consider engaging in gentle activities like yoga or stretching. Active recovery, such as low-intensity activities like walking or light stretching, can maintain mobility and reduce muscle stiffness. Ensuring proper technique and form during exercises is vital to minimise the risk of injuries and muscle spasms. Working with a certified personal trainer or attending exercise classes can help you learn proper form and technique. When using weights or other equipment, ensure that you use appropriate resistance and follow correct techniques to avoid strain.

By following these guidelines, women in their 40s can select and perform exercises that are safe and effective, helping to maintain overall health and prevent common issues associated with ageing.

References:

National Health Service (NHS), Moderate Intensity Exercise

Chapter 7: Embracing Your Next Chapter

Life is a journey filled with unique stages, each offering its own challenges, experiences, and valuable lessons. As busy mums, the way we nurture ourselves—physically, mentally, and emotionally—greatly impacts our overall quality of life. This journey isn't just about moving through the years; it's about the choices we make and the efforts we put into caring for ourselves, shaping not only our well-being but also our ability to thrive and enjoy each moment.

The Vibrancy of Youth

Maturity often brings a deeper appreciation for the balance between self-care and the many responsibilities we juggle as busy mums. With years of experience, we understand that while our energy levels might not match those youthful days, our strength lies in resilience and wisdom. This stage is about embracing our unique journey, focusing on our well-being, and making choices that support both our health and our family. It's easy to overlook self-care in the hustle of parenting, but we know that our physical and mental health is crucial for setting a positive example for our children. By prioritising healthy habits now, we can ensure we remain vibrant and capable of tackling whatever life throws our way, proving that caring for ourselves is an investment in our future and our families.

The 40s

Older age can be a wonderful time of reflection, wisdom, and, ideally, contentment for us mothers who have steered the ups and downs of family life. The way we experience this stage often hinges on how well we've cared for ourselves over the years. For those who have made health and well-being a priority, this can be a period filled with ease and comfort. Regular exercise helps us maintain muscle strength, flexibility, and balance, which are crucial for reducing the risk of falls and injuries as we age. A nutritious diet supports our bones, brain health, and immune system, helping us feel our best.

The ageing process naturally brings about changes in decreased mobility, changes in vision and hearing, and the need for more medical care but these changes do not have to lead to a decline in quality of life. Many older adults who have prioritised their health find that they can continue to engage in activities they love, maintain independence, and enjoy meaningful relationships. They experience a slower rate of cognitive decline, have fewer chronic illnesses, and often have a more positive outlook on life. Conversely, those who have neglected their health may face a different reality in old age. Chronic conditions such as heart disease, diabetes, and arthritis, often exacerbated by poor lifestyle choices earlier in life, can limit mobility and independence. Cognitive decline may be more pronounced, and the ability to enjoy life's simple pleasures may be diminished. The financial and emotional burden of managing multiple health issues can also take a toll, not only on the individual but also on their loved ones.

The 40s are often considered a significant midlife stage, where many individuals begin to notice changes in their body and appearance. This period marks a transition from the youthful vitality of earlier years to a stage where the effects of ageing start to become more apparent. These changes can be both physical and emotional, and they vary from person to person. However, with the right approach, these changes can be managed effectively, allowing individuals to continue feeling confident and healthy.

The Midlife Transition in the Next Chapter

Entering the 40s and beyond often brings about noticeable shifts in the body's functioning and appearance. Metabolism tends to slow down, leading to weight gain even with the same diet and exercise routine that once maintained a stable weight. Skin begins to lose some of its elasticity, leading to wrinkles and sagging, and hair may start to thin or turn grey. Hormonal changes, particularly in women who may be approaching menopause, can also contribute to changes in energy levels, mood swings, and shifts in body composition.

Additionally, muscle mass may begin to decrease, and bone density can start to decline, increasing the risk of osteoporosis. These changes are a natural part of ageing, but they can feel particularly pronounced as one moves into their 40s.

Ladies, you will be pleased to hear that all is not lost and below I will take you through ways to stay looking and feeling your best.

Managing the Changes in Body and Beauty

While the changes that come with ageing are inevitable, there are many strategies to manage and even mitigate their effects. Taking a proactive approach to health and wellness can help maintain a youthful appearance and strong, resilient body.

1. **Prioritise Nutrition**: A balanced diet becomes even more crucial in your mature age. Focus on nutrient-dense foods that support overall health, such as fruits, vegetables, lean proteins, whole grains, and healthy fats. Calcium and vitamin D are especially important for bone health, while antioxidants can help protect the skin from damage. Staying hydrated is also key, as it supports skin elasticity and overall bodily functions.

2. **Regular Exercise**: Incorporating regular physical activity into your routine is essential for managing weight, maintaining muscle mass, and supporting cardiovascular health. Strength training exercises are particularly beneficial in the 40s as they help counteract muscle loss and support bone density. Additionally, flexibility exercises like yoga or Pilates can help maintain mobility and reduce the risk of injury.

3. **Skincare Routine**: As skin begins to show signs of ageing, adjusting your skincare routine can help maintain a healthy, youthful appearance. Using products with retinoids can boost collagen production and reduce the appearance of fine lines and wrinkles. Sunscreen is also essential to protect against UV damage, which accelerates skin ageing. Moisturizing regularly helps keep the skin hydrated and reduces the appearance of dryness and dullness.

4. **Hair Care**: With potential changes in hair texture and colour, it's important to adapt your hair care routine. Using gentle shampoos and conditioners, as well as products designed for ageing hair, can help maintain hair health. If greying hair is a concern, exploring hair colour options however, embracing the natural change can be empowering.

5. **Hormonal Balance**: For women, the 40s often coincide with perimenopause, the transition period leading up to menopause. This stage can bring symptoms such as hot flashes, mood swings, and changes in menstrual cycles. Managing these symptoms can involve lifestyle changes. As we looked at earlier these do not have to be mega changes but exercise & meditation are perfect stress management techniques. Some women may also explore hormone replacement therapy (HRT) or other treatments in consultation with a healthcare provider.

6. **Mental and Emotional Well-being**: The 40s can also bring about emotional changes, sometimes referred to as a "midlife crisis." This period may prompt reflection on life choices, leading to stress or anxiety. Prioritising mental health through practices like mindfulness, meditation, or therapy can help navigate these emotional transitions. Staying connected with loved ones and maintaining a strong support system is also important for emotional well-being.

7. **Embracing Change**: Perhaps one of the most important aspects of managing the changes that come with ageing is embracing them with a positive mindset. Ageing is a natural process, and while it may bring changes that can feel challenging, it also comes with wisdom, experience, and the opportunity for personal growth. Focusing on self-acceptance and cultivating a sense of gratitude for what your body can still do can help you navigate this stage with confidence.

The Role of Self-Care Throughout Life

The concept of self-care is crucial throughout all stages of life. Self-care encompasses more than just physical health; it includes mental, emotional, and social well-being. It involves making conscious decisions to engage in behaviours that promote overall health and prevent illness. The importance of self-care cannot be overstated, as it plays a significant role in determining the quality of life in old age.

1. **Physical self-care**: engaging in regular physical activity, maintaining a balanced diet, staying hydrated, getting enough sleep, and avoiding harmful substances like tobacco and excessive alcohol are foundational to good health. These habits help maintain a healthy weight, reduce the risk of chronic diseases, and improve overall physical function.
2. **Mental and emotional self-care**: mental health is just as important as physical health. Practices like meditation, mindfulness, and stress management techniques can help maintain emotional balance. Regular mental challenges, such as puzzles, learning new skills, or engaging in creative activities, keep the mind sharp. Building strong, supportive relationships and seeking help when needed are also vital aspects of emotional self-care.
3. **Social Self-Care**: Maintaining social connections and engaging in meaningful activities contributes to a sense of purpose and belonging, which are essential for emotional well-being. Volunteering, joining clubs or groups, and staying connected with friends and family can provide social support and reduce the risk of loneliness, which is often a challenge in old age.
4. **Preventive Care**: Regular health check-ups, screenings are an important aspect of self-care. Preventive care helps catch potential health issues early, making them easier to manage and treat. It's also important to stay informed about health risks and take proactive steps to mitigate them.

The Payoff in Midlife

The efforts put into self-care throughout life pay off in old age in many ways. Older adults who have consistently cared for themselves often enjoy a higher quality of life. They are more likely to remain independent, with the ability to perform daily tasks and engage in activities they enjoy. They may experience fewer medical issues, lower healthcare costs, and less reliance on medication. Moreover, the psychological benefits of self-care are significant. Those who have taken care of their mental and emotional health tend to have a more positive outlook on life, better coping mechanisms for dealing with the challenges of ageing, and stronger relationships with family and friends. This leads to a greater sense of fulfilment and satisfaction in old age.

Your 40s are a pivotal decade for personal growth and self-care. Often, it's a time when life's responsibilities, career, family, health, and finances converge, demanding your attention. Amidst these demands, it's easy to lose sight of your own needs and well-being. However, this decade is not just about managing external factors; it's also about turning inward and prioritising yourself. By doing so, you can navigate this period with greater fulfilment, balance, and resilience.

Why Prioritising Yourself is Crucial

The maturity is often marked by an accumulation of responsibilities—career demands, parenting, caregiving for ageing parents, and financial planning. Without adequate self-care, the pressure from these responsibilities can lead to burnout, stress, and health issues. Prioritising yourself helps you recharge and maintain the energy needed to manage these demands effectively. Physical health can begin to show signs of wear and tear in your 40s. By focusing on your well-being now—through regular exercise, healthy eating, and stress management—you can prevent long-term health problems and maintain your vitality as you age.

Enhancing Emotional and Mental Well-being:

Life's challenges often intensify during this decade, requiring strong emotional resilience. Prioritising self-care practices such as meditation, therapy, or simply taking time for yourself can significantly enhance your emotional well-being and equip you to handle stress more effectively. The 40s are a time when many people reassess their lives. This introspection can lead to a renewed understanding of who you are and what you want out of life. Prioritising yourself allows you to explore your interests, passions, and goals, leading to greater satisfaction and a sense of purpose. By prioritising your own needs, you learn to set healthy boundaries in your relationships. This not only protects your well-being but also enhances the quality of your interactions with others, leading to more fulfilling and supportive relationships. As mothers we can never forget we have little ones who look up to us, prioritising self-care sets a powerful example. It teaches the importance of self-respect and the need to balance self-nourishment.

Living Fully, Living Well

The Beauty of a New Decade

As we step into our 40s, we enter a period of profound personal growth and transformation. It's a time when many of us begin to reflect more deeply on our lives, reassess our goals, and re-evaluate our priorities. For single mums, this decade can be particularly significant. It's a time to balance the demands of motherhood with personal aspirations and rediscover the parts of ourselves that may have been put on hold. You have a unique opportunity to redefine what success and happiness mean to you. The experience and wisdom you've gained over the years can serve as a solid foundation for making informed, empowered choices. Embracing this decade means acknowledging the strengths you've cultivated and using them to create a life that aligns with your true values and desires.

Balancing Career and Motherhood

One of the most significant challenges for any mother is balancing career ambitions with the responsibilities of raising their children. This balance can be difficult to achieve but is essential for personal fulfilment. Many women find that their maturity offers a chance to recalibrate their professional goals and find more meaningful ways to integrate their careers with their family lives.

Take time to assess your career goals. Are they still aligned with your current values and circumstances? Do you need to make adjustments to better suit your lifestyle? This period of life can be a time of reinvention, where you have the experience and confidence to pursue new opportunities or shift your focus to areas that bring greater satisfaction.

Celebrating Milestones

Recognizing Achievements

Milestones are more than just markers of time; they are celebrations of your journey, achievements, and growth. As you navigate your mature age, it's essential to recognize and honour these significant moments. Whether it's a personal accomplishment, a professional success, or a meaningful life event, each milestone deserves to be celebrated.

Take time to reflect on the milestones you've reached so far. Consider how each one has shaped you and contributed to your growth. Celebrating these moments not only boosts your self-esteem but also reinforces the progress you've made. It's a way to acknowledge your efforts, perseverance, and the challenges you've overcome.

Creating a Milestone Journal

To celebrate your milestones, consider incorporating this event into your journal or creating a journal solely dedicated to your achievements. Big or small, take note of how they've impacted your life. This practice can serve as a powerful reminder of your strength and resilience, inspiring you to continue pursuing your goals with determination and enthusiasm.

A milestone journal is not just a record of accomplishments; it's a tool for self-reflection and gratitude. As you jot down each milestone, take a moment to reflect on the journey that led you there. What challenges did you overcome? What lessons did you learn? How did this experience shape you? This reflective practice can deepen your appreciation for your progress and motivate you to keep moving forward.

Celebrating Personal Growth

Personal growth is a significant aspect of the milestones we celebrate in our mature age. This decade often brings a deeper understanding of ourselves and a greater sense of authenticity. Celebrate the moments when you've taken steps towards self-improvement, whether it's through personal development courses, therapy, or simply making time for self-care. These milestones of personal growth are equally important as external achievements. They represent your commitment to becoming the best version of yourself and living a life that aligns with your true values. Acknowledge these moments and take pride in the person you are becoming.

Practice Saying No:

Learning to say no is an important skill, especially in your maturity when demands on your time and energy are high. Setting boundaries allows you to protect your time and focus on what truly matters to you. Not everything requires your immediate attention. Prioritise activities that align with your goals and well-being, and let go of those that drain your energy without adding value to your life.

Shifting Your Mindset About Ageing

Embracing a Positive Perspective

For us women, ageing is often viewed through a negative lens in our society, but it doesn't have to be that way. Shifting your mindset about ageing can transform how you experience your maturity and beyond. Instead of focusing on the perceived limitations of ageing, embrace the opportunities it presents.

One way to shift your mindset is to adopt a perspective of gratitude. Recognize the advantages that come with age, such as increased self-awareness, emotional intelligence, and the ability to navigate life's complexities with greater ease. Each year brings new experiences and lessons that enrich your understanding of the world and yourself.

Challenging Societal Stereotypes

Another effective strategy is to challenge societal stereotypes about getting older. Surround yourself with positive role models who defy conventional notions of what it means to age. Seek out stories of individuals who have achieved remarkable feats in their later years, and let their examples inspire you to pursue your passions without fear or hesitation. Research shows that a positive attitude towards ageing can significantly impact your overall well-being. According to a study published in the Journal of Personality and Social Psychology, individuals with positive self-perceptions of ageing lived 7.5 years longer than those with less positive perceptions. This statistic underscores the power of mindset in shaping our experiences and outcomes.

Practising Mindfulness and Meditation

Try incorporating mindfulness exercises into your daily routine with simple practices like deep breathing, body scans, or guided meditation. These techniques can also enhance focus and help you stay grounded, bringing a sense of calm and clarity to your day.

The Benefits of Maturity and Experience

As you progress through your maturity, a profound realisation begins to take hold: the maturity and experience you've accumulated over the years are among your most powerful assets. As we delve further into how these qualities can enrich every aspect of your life, from personal growth to professional achievements and from deeper relationships to a more balanced perspective on life. The benefits of maturity and experience are invaluable, and understanding how to harness them will empower you to navigate this decade with confidence, wisdom, and fulfilment.

A Deeper Understanding of Yourself

As I previously stated, one of the most significant advantages of reaching your 40s is the deepened understanding of yourself that naturally develops over time. The journey through life thus far has likely been filled with a wide array of experiences—triumphs, setbacks, joys, and sorrows. These experiences have not only shaped your identity but have also brought you closer to understanding your true self. By now, you have a clearer sense of what truly matters to you. The values and priorities that guide your decisions have been honed through years of life experiences. This clarity allows you to align your actions with your core beliefs, leading to a more fulfilling and authentic life. The prime of life brings with it a greater sense of self-acceptance. In your younger years, you may have felt pressured to meet societal expectations or conform to others' standards. Now, in your maturity, there is a shift toward embracing who you are, imperfections and all. This self-acceptance is liberating and allows you to live more authentically, free from the constraints of perfectionism.

Enhanced Emotional Intelligence

With age comes a natural increase in emotional intelligence (EQ), a vital skill that enhances every area of life. Emotional intelligence involves the ability to understand and manage your emotions, as well as the capacity to empathise with others. Your enhanced emotional intelligence allows you to navigate complex interpersonal dynamics with greater ease. You are better equipped to manage conflicts, understand social cues, and foster deeper, more meaningful connections. This ability to connect on a deeper emotional level leads to more satisfying relationships, both personally and professionally. Emotional intelligence also plays a crucial role in how you handle stress. By now, you've likely developed strategies to manage stress effectively, whether through mindfulness practices, physical activity, or seeking support from trusted friends. These coping mechanisms help you maintain emotional balance even in the face of challenges.

Stronger Decision-Making Skills

Maturity significantly enhances your decision-making abilities. In your maturity, the process of making decisions becomes more thoughtful, deliberate, and informed, drawing on the rich tapestry of your life experiences. The experiences you've accumulated over the years serve as a valuable resource when faced with important decisions. You can reflect on past successes and mistakes, applying those lessons to present situations. This ability to draw on past experiences allows you to make more informed and confident choices. Maturity often brings a greater sense of patience. You are less likely to rush into decisions and more inclined to consider the long-term implications. This broader perspective enables you to make choices that are not only beneficial in the short term but also sustainable and aligned with your long-term goals.

Greater Resilience

Resilience is something we all develop over time, especially as busy mums who are constantly juggling personal and family challenges. By this stage in life, you've likely faced your fair share of ups and downs—whether it's been balancing work with raising children, managing a household, or overcoming personal hurdles. And with each challenge, you've grown stronger and more capable.

One of the key traits of resilience is adaptability—something we mums are pros at. Whether it's handling a sudden change in plans, managing the chaos of daily life, or adjusting to the emotional and physical shifts that come with this stage of life, you've learned to bend without breaking. This flexibility allows you to stay grounded and composed, even when things feel overwhelming.

Every obstacle you've overcome has built your confidence, reminding you that you can handle whatever comes next. And that self-assurance is a superpower! It helps you face new challenges with the belief that you have the strength, wisdom, and experience to get through them. Resilience doesn't mean you never struggle—it means you know how to rise, time and time again, with grace and determination.

More Meaningful Relationships

As we evolve, our relationships naturally become deeper and more meaningful. By this stage in life, especially as a busy mum, you've gained a clear understanding of what truly matters in your relationships and what you need from the people around you. You've likely learned how to cultivate connections that feel authentic and fulfilling—whether it's with friends, family, or even your partner.

At this point, you tend to be more selective about who you invest your time and energy in. After all, life is busy, and the relationships that really count are the ones that lift you up, bring joy, and offer genuine support. Surrounding yourself with people who add value to your life becomes a priority, and it's this intentional focus that makes your connections so much more enriching.

With the wisdom that comes from experience, your emotional intelligence has deepened, allowing you to connect with others in a more authentic way. You're better at understanding the emotional needs of your loved ones—whether it's your children, partner, or close friends—and this often leads to more satisfying and lasting relationships. The bonds you've nurtured over time have likely become stronger and more resilient, and these deep connections are especially important for maintaining that sense of balance and support in your life.

The Power of Perspective

One of the true gifts of maturity is gaining a sense of perspective that only comes with time and experience. By this stage in life, you've likely seen it all—the highs, the lows, and everything in between—and that gives you a broader, more balanced view of the world. As mums with hectic schedules, this perspective is invaluable because it helps you rise above the small daily stresses and see the bigger picture. You're less likely to get caught up in minor setbacks or temporary challenges because you've learned that life's bumps don't define your journey.

With this newfound clarity, you tend to focus more on your long-term goals and the overall direction of your life. Those short-term obstacles that might have thrown you off course in the past now seem less overwhelming. This ability to maintain perspective helps you stay grounded, focused, and clear about what truly matters to you.

At this point, with the benefit of hindsight and experience, it's easier to prioritise the things that bring real value to your life—whether that's your health, your relationships, or your own personal growth. The things that may have seemed important in your younger years, like material pursuits or trying to meet societal expectations, often fall by the wayside. This shift in focus is a natural and deeply rewarding part of life's journey, allowing you to lead a more balanced, content, and rewarding life.

Embracing Your Strengths

By this stage in life, you've gained a deep understanding of your strengths and how to use them to your advantage. As women, this self-awareness becomes a powerful tool, allowing you to focus on the things that truly align with your natural talents and abilities. Over the years, you've honed your skills, whether it's in your career, managing a household, or pursuing personal passions. This hard-earned experience brings with it a quiet confidence—whether you're handling a tricky project at work, leading a family event, or even diving into a new hobby. You know what you're good at, and you're no longer afraid to tackle challenges that let you shine.

Understanding your strengths also means knowing where to put your energy. With so many demands on your time, focusing on what you excel at helps you not only boost your productivity but also achieve a greater sense of satisfaction. After all, when you play to your strengths, you're more likely to succeed and feel a sense of accomplishment. By leveraging these abilities, you're able to lead a more purposeful and satisfying life, knowing that you're making the most of the skills and wisdom you've gained along the way.

Key Takeaways:

One of the most important lessons we learn as life gets busier is the need to prioritise ourselves. As mums, it's so easy to put everyone else's needs first, and before you know it, you're feeling burnt out, stressed, or even dealing with health issues. But focusing on self-care—whether that's regular exercise, eating well, or managing stress—becomes essential. It's an investment in your well-being, not just for your physical health, but for your emotional and mental resilience too. Life's demands can feel overwhelming at times, so finding practices that help you feel centred—like meditation, therapy, or simply carving out time for yourself—can make a huge difference. These habits help you manage the feelings of being overwhelmed more effectively and keep a balanced perspective.

This stage of life also brings a lot of introspection. You might find yourself reassessing your goals, passions, and the direction you want your life to take. With the wisdom that comes from experience, you're in a great position to redefine what success and happiness really means to you. This period often leads to a clearer understanding of your values, helping you make choices that feel more content and aligned with what truly matters. By focusing on what brings you joy and satisfaction, you create a deeper sense of purpose in your life.

Learning to set healthy boundaries becomes essential as your responsibilities grow. With so many demands on your time and energy, "saying No" when necessary is a vital skill. Setting boundaries isn't selfish; it's a way to protect your well-being and ensure that your time is spent on activities that truly align with your values and goals. By being more selective with where you invest your energy, you reduce unnecessary stress and enhance your overall quality of life.

Ageing often gets a bad reputation in society, but this stage offers a real opportunity to embrace it with positivity. Instead of focusing on what might be changing, it's important to appreciate the opportunities that come with growing older. A positive outlook can have a significant impact on your well-being and contribute to a longer, healthier life. As we covered, practices like mindfulness and meditation can help you stay calm and embrace ageing as a natural, enriching part of life.

Wisdom and experience are some of your greatest assets now. You likely have a deeper understanding of yourself, which helps you live more authentically and align your actions with your core beliefs. This maturity also brings stronger emotional intelligence, allowing you to navigate complex relationships with greater ease and form deeper, more meaningful connections. You can draw on past experiences to make confident decisions, and the resilience you've developed through life's challenges becomes a powerful tool for handling difficulties with grace. By focusing on your well-being, setting boundaries, celebrating your achievements, and maintaining a positive attitude toward ageing, you can approach this stage of life with confidence, balance, and fulfilment. The wisdom and strength you've gained will continue to guide you as you make empowered choices and create a more satisfying, authentic life.

References:
American Psychological Association, Journal of Personality and Social Psychology

Closing Remarks

As we come to the conclusion of this journey together, I hope you feel empowered and inspired to embrace balance in your busy lives as mothers. Balancing the demands of family, work, and self-care can often feel like a high-wire act—one moment, you're acing your work presentation, and the next, you're navigating a toddler tantrum. It can be overwhelming, but let's remember that finding this balance is not just essential for your well-being; it's also crucial for your children's growth and development.

Life as a busy mum is filled with countless responsibilities, from school runs and meal prep to managing playdates and household chores. In the midst of this whirlwind, it's easy to lose sight of your needs and desires. But here's the secret: when you prioritise your own health and happiness, you're better equipped to support your family. Think of yourself as the foundation of a house; if that foundation is strong and secure, the entire structure can stand tall.

By demonstrating a balanced approach to work and play, you're teaching your children some of life's most valuable lessons. They are observant little beings; they soak up everything around them. When they see you navigating your commitments with grace, taking time for yourself, and still engaging fully with them, you're instilling in them the importance of balance. This is not just about managing time; it's about creating a lifestyle where both structured activities and free play thrive. Such an environment fosters creativity and independence in your kids, allowing them to explore their interests and develop critical thinking skills.

So, how do we make this happen amidst the chaos? Let's talk about practical strategies. **Creating a structured routine** is one of the most effective ways to ensure that everyone's needs are met. Establish a daily schedule that includes dedicated time for schoolwork, chores, extracurricular activities, and—yes—free play for everyone in the family. For you, set specific times for your work tasks and family interactions, ensuring a clear distinction between work time and family time. This structured approach doesn't just help you stay organised; it also teaches your children valuable time-management skills.

Prioritising tasks together can be a wonderful bonding experience. Encourage your children to list their tasks and activities in order of importance. This not only empowers them to take responsibility but also allows you to model the behaviour you wish to instil. By prioritising your tasks, you demonstrate how to balance urgent work tasks with family needs effectively.

Another strategy is to **integrate learning into play**. Incorporate educational games and activities that blend fun with learning. Cooking together can teach maths and science concepts while creating lasting memories. These moments of shared learning are invaluable for both you and your children.

Now, let's discuss **screen time**—we all know how easy it is to get lost in our devices. Setting boundaries for screen time is crucial for both you and your children. Limit their screen exposure and make sure it doesn't interfere with physical activity, social interaction, or sleep. Use this time wisely; engage in activities that foster connection and joy.

Encouraging independent play is another effective strategy. Allow your children to engage in unstructured, self-directed play. This fosters creativity and problem-solving skills while giving you precious time to engage in self-care activities. Use this time for yourself—whether that's enjoying a bubble bath, catching up on a favourite show, or simply savouring a quiet moment with a cup of tea.

Family time is equally important. Dedicate regular time for family activities that everyone can enjoy together, like board games, outdoor adventures, or creative projects. Make it a point to be fully present during these moments. Put away your phone, switch off the work email, and soak in the laughter and joy of being together. It's during these moments that the magic happens, and you build those lasting family memories.

Teaching time management to your children will benefit them greatly as they grow. Use visual schedules and timers to help them see how to allocate their time effectively. Apply these same techniques to your tasks; break larger projects into manageable steps, and don't forget to take breaks!

As you help your children balance their extracurricular activities, remember to choose options that align with their interests and strengths, but avoid overloading their schedules. Flexibility is key—not just in your children's activities but in your own schedule as well. Life with little humans is unpredictable, and being adaptable will not only reduce pressure on you but also teach your children how to handle changes with grace.

Promoting physical activity is essential for everyone in the family. Ensure your children have ample opportunities for physical exercise, whether through sports, dance, or simply playing outside. For yourself, find ways to incorporate physical activity into your routine. This could mean family walks, fun dance parties in the living room, or solo workouts that rejuvenate you.

Don't forget the importance of **communicating the value of balance**. Regularly discuss with your children why balance is important and how it benefits their overall well-being. Encourage them to reflect on their activities and feelings. Ask them whether they feel balanced and what changes might help improve that.

Remember, your children's needs will evolve as they grow. Adapt your approach to maintaining balance, recognizing that what works now may need to shift later. Celebrate their achievements as they learn to balance responsibilities and playtime; acknowledgment fosters motivation and encourages further growth.

As you embark on this journey, set **realistic expectations** for yourself. Perfection is a myth! Some days will be more balanced than others, and that's completely okay. Delegate **tasks** whenever possible. Share household responsibilities with your partner and children. This not only teaches teamwork and responsibility but also helps lighten your load.

Use **technology wisely**; leverage apps and tools for scheduling, reminders, and managing family activities to stay organised. Create a **support network** by connecting with other mums for support, advice, and sharing responsibilities like babysitting. And of course, don't forget to plan ahead—preparing meals in advance, laying out clothes the night before, and keeping a family calendar can significantly make time for what matters.

Lastly, always prioritise taking care of yourself. A healthy, happy mum can better support her family. Be kind to yourself and recognize that self-care isn't selfish; it's necessary.

As you implement these strategies, remember that you are not just managing responsibilities; you are modelling the importance of balance to your children. By creating a harmonious family environment where both work and play are valued, you're ensuring that your family thrives.

Here's to you, busy mums! May you find joy in the beautiful chaos of motherhood and discover that balance is not just a destination but a rewarding journey. Embrace it fully, and watch how it transforms your life and your family for the better. Together, let's create a legacy of balance, resilience, and joy for generations to come!

About the Author

Sommer Currie is a certified NLP & Empowerment Mindset Coach dedicated to supporting women in unlocking their full potential. Specialising in working with entrepreneurs, creatives, mums, and business leaders, Sommer empowers her clients to overcome barriers, conquer self-doubt, and break free from limiting beliefs. Her personalised approach helps women find clarity, direction, and purpose in their personal and professional lives.

Sommer would love to hear about your experience with this book. If it resonated with you or provided valuable insights, please consider leaving a review. Your feedback not only helps others discover the book but also supports its mission of empowering more women.

For more information and resources, visit www.sommercurrie.com.

Acknowledgments;

I would like to extend my heartfelt gratitude to Muhammad Muheaman for their invaluable creative editorial skills, which played a significant role in shaping this book. Your guidance and expertise have been a true gift.

Printed in Great Britain
by Amazon